An American Soldier's Korean Journey

Donald Ray Borgman

Korean War Veteran

Self-published by Donald Ray Borgman
Grand Junction, CO
Printed in the United States via CreateSpace.com

Permission for the use of text and photos has been diligently sought, and every effort has been made to record accurate names and historical information. Should there be any errors or omissions, corrections will gladly be made in future publishing.

Grateful acknowledgment is made to Michael Hickey for permissions to reprint text excerpts from *The Korean War* copyright © 1999 Michael Hickey. Published in 2000 by The Overlook Press, New York, New York. All rights reserved.

Grateful acknowledgment is made to the veterans who generously contributed their accounts at the 2006 Korean War Veteran's Reunion in Mesquite, NV and permit reprinting of text excerpts from the transcripts. The accounts spoken at the 2006 Korean Vet's Reunion were transcribed mainly for the benefit of our hearing impaired friends. However, copies may be freely distributed to any interested friends who were not able to attend, or others who may enjoy them. If copies are made in whole or in part, please include this text. Please pardon transcription errors. The several transcribers attempted to convey in words, the feelings and thoughts expressed by each speaker. Most of the accounts are verbatim, except that some "ahs," "ands," repeats, and such were left out to enhance readability. Some added comments, enclosed in [], have been added to enhance the "flavor," the feeling of "being there," for indexing the book, and/or to explain things that happened that were not reflected in the recordings. The notation [_??] is used to indicate possibly significant undecipherable words from the audio recordings (themselves not perfect) which were transcribed. A reasonable attempt was made to proofread each account; however, errors may still exist. Where the correct spelling of names and places could not be determined, a phonetic spelling was used. Errata will be placed at http://rkivs.com/kwvr/transcripts_errata.html if corrections are found after printing.

ISBN: 978-1442191198
EAN-13:   9781442191198

Dedication

This book is dedicated to my beautiful wife, Joann. She has become my life and reason for pressing on. She is the one who inspired me to begin writing and encouraged me to continue when the project seemed daunting. She contributed patience, advice, and immense enthusiasm. Often her prompting brought to mind memories that otherwise might have been forgotten. Joann has worked by my side continually helping me find the words to express my thoughts. Over the years she has sought ways to help me deal with war memories in a positive way. Writing this book has been tremendously helpful. Without her, this book and its beneficial effects could never have come to fruition.

Table of Contents

Table of Contents

Epilogue

Prologue

Many times over the years I reminisced about my experiences in Korea. The thoughts and memories are not always easy. But, in the process of time, I found purpose for the experience. Now I can truly say, "I am honored to be a Korean War veteran."

Recently, I am more comfortable talking about the events and sharing stories regarding my service in the Korean War. Interest in these accounts of war history has been expressed by more people than I imagined. They are genuinely intrigued by my story.

People are interested in obtaining a better understanding, a glimpse, of the cost of freedom. Now I appreciate the interest, and I am pleased to share my stories, even though I believe only veterans fully understand another veteran. Without the shared experience it is impossible to really know how the unimaginable has shaped an individual's perspective. Yet, many people want to know. They want to know what individual veterans accomplished to keep alive the hopes and values of our great nation.

Perhaps former President Franklin Roosevelt expressed it best when he said:

> *In all of the far flung operations of our armed forces the toughest job has been performed by the average, easy going, hard fighting young American, who carries the weight of the battle on his young shoulders. It is to him that we and all future generations must pay grateful tribute. (Franklin Delano Roosevelt, January 6, 1945, State of the Union Address)*

Official recognition is an important and necessary part of grateful tribute. However, it is incomplete without more understanding. A genuine interest in what was done is rich meaningful tribute. It has occurred to me that some people may not really know how to ask. How do you approach a veteran and inquire about their experience? Some may wonder if it will inflict more pain. There was a time when that was true. Now I wish to write about my story, to share without reserve my memories, and include how I discovered purpose. My initial motivation was to have my story be known by my extended family. As I began talking openly about my experiences, it became clear that there is a broader interest. Now is the time to share with others the reasons I am honored to be a Korean War veteran.

The Beginning of the Story

Chapter 1
Getting Started

Where do I begin? This is an account of many separate stories. Telling stories goes beyond preserving history. Personal accounts give insight into what shapes our perspectives, values and culture. There was a time in history when an incredibly important story was lost with the passing of generations: the story of Exodus. Judges 2:10 describes a generation that lost the story of deliverance from Egypt into the Promised Land. As a result, they were greatly disadvantaged.

Perhaps I will start with the title of this book: *An American Soldier's Korean Journey*. For me it has truly been a journey: a lifetime of collective experiences. What I experienced later in life helped me better understand and appreciate my life as a young soldier. It has been said, to those who have served in the military, "life has a special flavor that the protected people will never know" (Office of Insular Affairs, para. 12). In telling my story, I hope to relate a measure of a veteran's perspective; to communicate the value of the veteran.

This is a historical account of young men doing what was necessary during a frightening time. We embraced the limits of our courage, fears, strength and endurance. It is a part of our lives that we remember both as the best and worst of times. Many soldiers lived in unexplainable conditions. Heights of adventure accompanied equally heavy burdens of hardship, tragedy and loss. The Korean War was fought at a time in history when war was still conducted as close-in combat.

The casualties and destructiveness of the war are shockingly costly. However, this book is also about the purpose; why this part of history continues to be meaningful. My vested interest in Korea helps me see benefits I would otherwise likely not know. Today there remains a stark contrast between North and South Korea. The south is free, prosperous and progressing. They are making a positive contribution on a global scale. It is also a place where freedom has allowed many people to enjoy a rich open fellowship in the gospel of Jesus Christ. It is clear to me now that freedom is always worth protecting even when it is very costly.

As we reflect upon our history, we better understand how the intensity of war activities completely obscured the greater purpose we understand today. We, who have served in the defense of our nation, understand the intricacies of national security. A response is required to those who threaten this great country and consider us an enemy. Today it is easy to indulge ourselves in our lifestyles while giving little thought to the threats to our national security. Those with courage and willingness to serve their country have earned a great honor.

Writing this book will allow my children, grandchildren and future generations to know what I experienced as a soldier in the Korean War. I want to provide understanding for the purpose of standing up against tyranny and the value in making a stand for freedom. Some long-lasting benefits may not be realized until many years later. I want my family to know I am honestly thankful my country called upon me to serve in the Korean War. Perhaps this will further extend the bond between our family, our great country and the Korean people. Now I am really getting ahead of myself; let's get started.

Chapter 2
Growing Up

My story begins with my paternal grandfather and the Borgmann family. A shipwreck brought him to America and thus our family became Americans. My father often told an interesting story about grandfather's United States immigration process. Employed by a German shipping company, my grandfather sailed from Germany. His ship sank leaving only three survivors; my grandfather and two other men. After several days in a lifeboat, another ship rescued them. While I do not know the destination of the ship that sank, the rescuing ship was on course to New York; the determining factor in my grandfather's immigration.

Both of my father's parents were from Germany. My mother's parents, the Koening family, emigrated from Holland.

Borgmann and Koening Grandparents (family photos)

These two families settled in northern Illinois. On July 20, 1929, I was born in a home south of Freeport; the only child of Joe and Gertie Borgman (my father changed the spelling of his last name by dropping the last letter). While I remember my Koening grandparents well, my Borgmann grandparents passed away prior to my birth.

Rear patio of the house where I was born - 1931 (family photo)

Dad, Mom and me – 1935 (family photo)

We remained in Freeport until I was five years old then moved to Baileyville. It was our American dream; a bit of property, a house, dog and cat, and summer evenings on the porch. There were family and friends. My dog, Fritzie, and I

were great buddies.   So much so my nick name became
Fritzie for many years. Yes, there were all the usual financial
concerns that accompany family life and worries about World
War II. Yet, freedom felt so natural.

My school and class (D'Anca, p. 87, 105)

I attended eight years of school in a schoolhouse across
the street from where we lived. It was a two story building,
but all eight grades were taught in one room. Our teacher,
Mrs. Anna Borchers, was a kind person and she was highly
regarded as an outstanding teacher. Another teacher came
and helped us during my last couple school years. More
children had moved into our area and the crowded school
conditions became too much for one teacher. After finishing
grammar school, I continued on to high school in Foreston,
about a five mile bus ride from home. When I was 13, I
began working part-time on a farm and enjoyed it very much.
I graduated when I was 17 and began working full-time on
the farm where I drove tractors and helped with other farm
equipment. I was making money and did not worry about
school anymore.

Many times during these years I remember my mother
and father talking with relatives about World War II. My
parents were very concerned, great fear accompanied
thoughts of war, yet I did not understand much about their

concerns. My employer, the farmer and his family, also talked often about World War II.

I was at work the day the atomic bomb hit Japan, and I also remember clearly that August day in 1945 when Japan surrendered. My employer and his family were overjoyed. They came and told me the news, and said we would quit work early. I was invited to accompany them to Freeport and celebrate victory. We found the streets in both directions full of cars; horns blared with triumph. The soldiers and their girlfriends were in high spirits. Everyone was weary from war and a victory celebration was just what people needed. Little did I know I would be called upon in a few short years to serve my country; making a stand against tyranny on foreign soil.

Chapter 3
Called to Korea

As required by the United States Army, I registered for the military draft in Freeport when I was 18. During the registration process I was asked to report for a physical exam. I traveled by train from Oregon, IL to Chicago for the procedure. The results soon arrived in the mail; a 1A physical classification meaning there was nothing physically wrong with me and I was eligible to be a soldier. I was officially registered.

However, I soon realized I was not registered as a conscientious objector (CO) which required a form with written explanation. Submitting the form let the draft board know I would not bear arms and kill a person. Later I received a new classification of 1AO. The "O" indicated I was a conscientious objector.

The CO classification is a special and considerate provision offered by our military. A couple of our ministers made a special effort to ensure that people of our faith could use this provision. Carl Linderman explained this effort in the account he contributed to the 2006 Korean War veteran's book.

Whenever it was mentioned about this great country of ours, we as veterans can appreciate it more than other veterans because this country provided us with the privilege of being conscientious objectors. What country facing what we faced in World War II could have done that? I remember George Walker telling us at a convention just after the outbreak of hostilities that he and Andrew Abernethy and maybe others, but those two men went to Washington and talked to the head of the Selective Service System, a man by the name of General Hershey and explained about our group, and General Hershey listened attentively and then he told them, "It takes seven men to keep one man on the front lines, and if you people are willing to do that we will appreciate it. "That is how it started for us to be conscientious objectors. And then think of this great country. That after they made provision for us to be COs we still had all the privileges of a regular veteran!! (KWVR, p. 14)

A short time after completing the registration and getting reclassified as a CO, I was drafted into the United States Army. I well remember the Saturday evening I came home from work and my mother handed me my mail. Inside an official looking envelope was a letter that began with the large word, "GREETINGS," followed by words similar to, "You have been selected by your neighbors and friends to join in the Army of your country to fill a place of protection against the threat of communism."

At the time I was employed by Klassy Milling Company hauling grain to barges on the Mississippi River and Lake Michigan. When I told my employer I received my draft notice for induction into the Armed Forces, he discussed the possibility of deferment because he had an agricultural related business. I thanked him for the offer, but told him that I was not interested. Being drafted stirred a strong sense of patriotic duty within me and I wanted to go and serve. I explained that I was ready and willing to serve with my country's military to provide protection against communism.

At the time it simply seemed like the right thing to do. I had no way of knowing what it really meant, but that decision marked the beginning of my Korean journey. It led to many experiences which expanded my horizons, formed a bond with another nation of people and ultimately enriched my life. Looking back I feel I had spiritual help making the decision. It led to many experiences that are still difficult to talk about, yet I am now grateful for the answer I gave my employer that day.

Korea was not a well known place for most of us young boys who had never left the shores of the United States. We began to hear many accounts of the conditions in Korea. It was shocking to read about a nation that was humiliated and impoverished by forty years of Japanese occupation, and now assaulted and shattered by an invasion from North Korea. We heard of its filth, its offensive odors, and how the majority of the population lived in poverty. It was also the first war to be fought with the acknowledged threat of nuclear attack. Fear of communist North Korea's invasion caused thousands of families to become refugees and flee their homes with only the possessions they could carry. It seemed so pitiful. My country called for my service and I felt duty-bound to go.

I was asked to report to Fort Sheridan, Chicago for military duty on April 5, 1951. My cousin, Don Meyers, took me to Oregon, IL to get on the train that morning. My father cried as I left.

When I arrived at Fort Sheridan, I was inducted into the Army of the United States of America. Upon my arrival, I vividly remember seeing a poster in a very large room that read: "KILL OR BE KILLED." It seemed like the letters were at least three feet tall. Every soldier has these two choices facing him.

At this camp we were not permitted to go out beyond the gates. If we somehow escaped, there would be punishment. Separation from the civilian world kept soldiers focused on their training and reduced distractions. Partying, of course, hindered our ability to fulfill a soldier's obligations. Isolation from "going to town" was difficult for the boys who were not familiar with following orders from direct authority.

Families could visit soldiers during scheduled times at camp, and my mother and father came to see me one time.

My first United States of America military uniform
Issued at Fort Sheridan (family photos)

Father, me and mother at Fort Sheridan (family photo)

Me and Don Myers at Fort Sheridan (family photo)

We were issued all our clothes at Fort Sheridan. Fatigues, class "A" uniform, combat boots and all. I soon realized that the Army had only two sizes of clothes: one size was too big, and the other was too small. That became my new wardrobe in its entirety. We were not permitted to wear any civilian clothes in or out of our camp, so I sent all my civilian clothes back home to my mother.

Life in the military had begun. One could hardly imagine what lay ahead, and it was impossible to understand the purpose of it all. Yet a patriotic sense of duty prevailed.

Hal Terrell, a World War II veteran, summarized the honor of serving when he wrote: "The office of a soldier is an honorable estate, for it is upon the willingness of the soldier sustained by the fellowship and discipline of the troops, to enter into mortal danger. It is upon his readiness to risk his very life that order and peace itself ultimately depends" (Terrell, p. 20). This expresses how I felt about the responsibility to serve my country. Standing up for your nation's freedom is an admirable duty, but to help other nations become free is even more admirable.

I felt ready and anxious to begin serving my country as a CO. These feelings were spurred by an underlying patriotism and sense of duty. Without knowing what was ahead, I began down a path of commitment and wanted to help a cause. Now, I feel strongly that it is a great honor to be a 1AO. I am reminded again of a common sentiment among soldiers: "for those who are willing to fight and die for freedom, life has a special flavor the protected will never know" (Office of Insular Affairs, para. 12). I was an American soldier who began the first leg of his Korean journey.

Preparing For Service

Chapter 4
A Good Reason to be Well Prepared

Freedom is not free. The costly fight for freedom is exemplified by the Korean War. When I left home, there was no possible way for me to comprehend the destructiveness of war. I was scheduled for basic training in preparation for service. However, we could never have fully prepared for what we eventually faced. We just took it one step at a time, did the best we knew how, and continually adjusted to the situation at hand. The combined adjustments became a series of escalations in my Korean War experience. Obligation began with induction and intensified through the rigors of basic training. Deployment to Korea amplified my commitment and all my duty together eventually climaxed with shocking frontline events. Each escalation had its costs for me, and overall the war extracted a tremendous toll in human lives and national treasure.

Volumes are published about the Korean War, but I appreciate the great summary by Ron Rudolph. It provides overall context for the situation.

KOREAN WAR SUMMARY
By Ron Rudolph

The Korean War was one of the most destructive wars of the 20th century. And yet it is often referred to as the "forgotten war." We need to ask ourselves how could it be forgotten when over 54,000 American soldiers died over there? Over 103,000 were seriously injured and removed from combat. There was over 3,000 of our American soldiers that died in Prisoner of War camps. Also, close to four million Koreans that died in that – they call it a "conflict!" Over four million Koreans! And over one million Chinese soldiers died. A lot of that happened in a three year period. There was a lot of hostility even after the signing of the cease fire – a lot of hostility and I do not mean to trivialize any portion of that war. But it is one not to be forgotten. You might ask how did the Korean War start. From 1910 to 1945 Japan essentially occupied and annexed the country of Korea. I believe its people were forbidden by the Japanese to speak the language and to write in Korean. Thirty-five years! Then at the conclusion of WWII the Russians wanted a part of it and the Americans would not permit them to take it all so they both assumed post-war responsibility for Korea. And that responsibility was divided at the 38th parallel. The Russians indoctrinated the North with their Communism and built up their military while in the south the US tried to help that country rebuild and form a democracy. In 1948 after several attempts to reunify that country, these South Koreans declared the Republic of Korea, and the North proclaimed the People's Republic of Korea. That was in 1948. In 1949 fighting began along the borders of that demilitarized zone, the DMZ, the 38th parallel. Then in 1950 on June 25th at four in the morning, the North Koreans began artillery and mortar barrages of South Korean positions, four A.M. in the morning. And 90,000 North Koreans with 150 Russian tanks came across that 38th parallel in a coordinated assault. That very day President Truman called on the United Nations. We were fresh out of WWII and the UN was to be the answer to a lot of our problems. He called on the UN to take police action against North

Korea. That next day fighter aircraft gave protective cover to the ships in Incheon Harbor while American citizens were being evacuated. That same day seven transports, air transports arrived at the Seoul airport with fighter cover. [Two of our ministers,] Uncle Sproulie and Uncle Don left on the second transport. Those transports were attacked by the North Korean air force and three of them were shot down to be the first aerial victories in that conflict. By day the North Koreans were already at the gates of Seoul when those transports left. By the fourth day, Seoul had fallen to the North Korean forces. And over the next 30 days, our boys desperately tried to stop the advances of the North Koreans. And at the end of those 30 days, they found themselves dug in the southeast corner of that country in the Port of Pusan. They were given orders to stand or die. It was a desperate situation. The North Koreans, if they could have gained that Port of Pusan, would have had control of the complete country. So for six weeks they threw everything they had at those UN and US soldiers that were trying to keep that territory. A few weeks later on September 15, General Douglas McArthur landed troops at Incheon and that was the turning point in that desperate situation – one of the turning points. The supply lines were cut, Seoul was recaptured and came under the control of the UN forces and there was very swift offensive advance across the 38th parallel and they were heading for the Yalu river when 300,000 Chinese crossed that river and with the North Koreans they drove our troops back on the defensive again. This time they recaptured Seoul, the second time, and that offensive was held about 70 miles south of Seoul when General Ridgeway and American troops started another offensive north. Can you imagine the desperate chaos, the desperate situation the Korean people found themselves in? When they were driven from their homelands looking for safety, looking for shelter, looking for food and here these armies are seesawing back and forth across Seoul. General Ridgeway headed north and the troops called that effort the "meat grinder" because of the casualties to the Chinese and North Koreans primarily, but there were casualties on our side too. This time they made it back to the 38th parallel, recaptured Seoul, back to the 38th parallel and for two years they seesawed back and forth across the 38th parallel. There were efforts made to get a cease fire and there were agreements and failures of agreements and then the aerial bombing was intensified, there was threat of the use of nuclear force and finally a cease fire and agreement was signed. That was in July 27, 1953. And from that point, guerrilla warfare was still very much a threat and in one period there were 7400 South Koreans killed, that was after the cease fire. (KWVR, p. 28)

This war amassed sobering statistics and astonishing costs. The numbers themselves are so large it is difficult to grasp the reality of the devastation. War veterans and people directly affected by the war read these statistics with perspective relating to their own war experiences. However, other civilians have difficulty fully understanding a veteran's perspective as well as the lasting effects of the war. The "road" must be explored and experienced to truly be understood.

Casualty figures below came from Carl Linderman.

- Korean veterans   1,800,000
- American soldiers who died   54,000
- American soldiers wounded in action   103,000
- Soldiers that became prisoners of war   8,177
- American soldiers who died in war
  prison camps   3,000
- Missing in action   12,616
- Korean civilians who died in the war   4,000,000
- South Koreans killed after the cease fire
  of July 1953   7,400

(KWVR, p. 28-29)

Michael Hickey also provides some astonishing figures. His information below represents 37 months of war.

- United Nation forces deployed   5,700,000

The US Navy

- Number of sorties flown from carrier
  aircraft   275,912

The US Air Force

- Strategic sorties flown   700,000
- Tactical sorties flown   625,000
- US Air Force lost aircrew   1,200
- Enemy aircraft destroyed   1,500
- MiGs aircraft destroyed   808
- MiGs aircraft damaged   925
- Enemy troops killed   145,416
- Enemy vehicles destroyed   74,589
- Pieces of railway destroyed   9,417

South Korean Rock Army:

- Killed in action   46,000
- Wounded   101,300
- Missing   12,000

Chinese Army:

- Killed   401,000
- Wounded   486,995
- Captured   21,211

North Korean Army:

- Killed   214,401
- Wounded   303,685
- Missing   101,680

(Hickey, p. 366)

Equally astounding was the amount of ammunition used in a short period of time. In September, 1951, about the time I arrived in Korea, the American 2nd Division's artillery alone fired off 153,000 rounds. One of its battalions achieved a record output of 14,425 rounds from 24 guns in 24 hours (Army Logistics University, para. 29).

The firing rate amounted to roughly one round every 2.4 minutes from each gun in an ongoing barrage. It effectively halted a Chinese advance and bought critical time for the UN troops to prepare further action. In the spring of 1952, the Chinese built up their artillery and deployed 900 guns in the forward areas. They fired 2,400 rounds a day.

Reading the summary and reviewing the statistics emphasizes the importance of preparation and training. Everyone in Korea suffered. Two million civilians perished in North Korea, representing 20 percent of the total population. In addition to the wounded and killed, there were thousands of prisoners, and many of them faced unimaginable conditions. "Some veterans of the Korean War contend that somewhere in North Korea, or Manchuria, American captives were never declared by the North Korean and Chinese authorities" (Hickey, p. 346). It is hard to know if this is true, yet given the war's brutality, it is understandable why veterans may feel this way. A great deal was lost, even for those who survived.

The war began on June 25, 1950 while I was employed as a truck driver in northern Illinois. John Muccio, a United States Ambassador in Seoul, heard the first air raids. He immediately drafted an evacuation plan for Americans and other foreign nationals. This was the only contingency plan America drafted for Korea. The North Korean Air Force effortlessly achieved immediate air superiority. Some

Americans were air-lifted out of Korea in between the frequent and unopposed air raids. It was during this time that our ministers, Sproulie Denio and Don Garland, were evacuated on the second transport. I find it interesting to think that they escaped safely in a very dangerous situation. On June 26, most remaining Americans and other civilians boarded an overcrowded Norwegian ship at Inchon.

The invasion of South Korea by the North Koreans was viewed by the world as an unprovoked aggression. Furthermore, Moscow was an assumed supporter of the invasion. In October 1950, Chinese troops were ordered across the Yalu River to support North Korea. The Chinese Army was accustomed to moving on foot with few motor vehicles. I was still at home while all of this took place, wondering when I would be called up for service.

The earliest engagement of US troops in Korea confirmed the importance of rigorous and disciplined training. While in Japan on occupation duty when the war started, the 24th Infantry Division deployed to Korea on July 1, 1950. However, unfortunately for them, they were not prepared for war. "Korea proved to be a dreadful shock to those inexperienced soldiers. Fewer than 10 percent had experienced combat. Some did not know how to clean their rifles or how to fire them. Some soldiers forgot to pull safety pins before they threw their grenades which provided the enemy with weapons to throw back" (Hickey, p. 165).

The Korean war started during the time we were still celebrating the victory of World War II and unprepared for another war. "During the first weeks of war, North Korea began taking prisoners. Thus, as American troops arrived piecemeal from Japan, hundreds fell into North Korean hands. The able-bodied were herded away and the sick and wounded left to die at the roadside; or murdered on the spot. North Koreans lavished no medical care on their prisoners as they forced them to march north. Hundreds simply laid down by the road and died" (Hickey, p. 338).

The harsh winter of late 1950 further complicated the situation and the bitter cold took its toll. During the night of January 12, 1951, the temperature dipped to -36 degrees. Sickness increased and life became a simple question of survival. In the numbing cold and with frozen feet, questions were being raised about fighting in Korea; war seemed obscure and for a worthless cause. The early lack of preparation had a wide range of effects. It was nearly impossible to see beyond the madness when the situation was exhausting and hope seemed distant.

The need for adequate preparation became painfully evident. Training could not guarantee survival; yet, survival depended on the coordinated and effective operations that training produced. Looking back on what I faced during those next couple years, I am very grateful for every bit of preparation.

Chapter 5
Infantry Basic Training

I was inducted into the Army at Fort Sheridan, IL, but infantry basic training took place at Fort Leonard Wood, MO. Basic supplies were distributed during the short stay at Fort Sheridan, then a troop train transferred new soldiers to Fort Leonard Wood, MO. The trip to Missouri seemed exceptionally long. Army life began and all was very different from what a young farm boy had ever thought or seen; so unlike civilian life.

I distinctly remember my concern while traveling to infantry training where we were trained to fight and kill. Uneasiness loomed as I pondered how the ranks and brass would react and treat me as a CO. I worried day and night about the difficulty of holding up under the pressures of military life and command. It was all so unfamiliar. I did not know at the time, but my CO classification would be completely ignored. Welcome to the military. Later I would learn that this experience was preparing me in an unintended way. I was learning to deal with situations outside of my control, yet keep myself together.

Basic training began at Fort Leonard Wood in classic military style. No passes. No going home to mother or wife. Everything was done by command. We worked our way around obstacles and did as we were told. Being ordered to the medical building for shots is a classic example. The boy ahead of me began to faint and went down. We picked him up, laid him where he would not be in the way and the line moved on. Command was given for meals, marches, bed time, reveille, pushups, and everything else. All the severe discipline taught us to respond to authority and be effective soldiers. None of it really tested my CO classification, but that came later.

The dreaded night arrived when the sergeant came to distribute rifles. We were instructed to line up to receive a rifle, and then to memorize our rifle number. A line was formed in the barracks and each soldier was given a rifle as they passed by the sergeant. When the sergeant tried to hand me a rifle, I refused to take one and proceeded to explain that I was a CO. I am sure this sergeant had never heard the words "conscientious objector" before, or since, or any other words that long. He was actually fairly young, but he was tough and had a strong command of foul language. That was my first exposure to being different in the Army. I mean exposure in every sense of the word. The next morning when we fell-out for formation, I was the only one without a weapon. The men were trained to march and stand at attention with a rifle. I was in my correct position among them along with all the right movements, but without a weapon. Then someone decided to give me a broom with several rolls of toilet paper on the stick. And so, that was my "rifle." The toilet paper did come in handy on long marches, however.

By this time, I received some "exposure" from the officers because I did not have a rifle. Many of the soldiers had no regard for the standard I was upholding and the pressures began to intensify. However, there was one boy in all the ranks who understood that I was harassed by both the officers and the troops. He talked with me one evening with words of comfort and encouragement. He told me, "Do not give in. They cannot make you take a rifle if that is your belief, and it is in the Constitution of The United States of America that you have the right to refuse a rifle!" That certainly meant a lot to me, and I wondered many times if that was help coming from heaven. There were 250 soldiers in my company and this was the only boy who helped me.

One day, I was called in before a panel of officers: a captain, a lieutenant, a chaplain, a sergeant and more. They all tried to convince me to take a rifle. When asked what denomination I belonged to, I answered, "Christian." They replied, "Every one of us here are Christians. We all believe in Jesus." I explained that our faith does not have a denominational name, because that is what the bible teaches us. That discussion did not help matters at all. Yet, I stayed with the simple principles and truths that I had been taught, and they finally let me go. Imagine it: Farm Boy vs. Military Authority! It was a very hard experience for me to be placed under such pressure. The officers were upset with me and they did not behave with kind gentleness. They treated me as if I were dumb and ignorant, and talked to me as though school had done nothing for me. Times like this left no doubt that the Christ Spirit within can indeed be strong and overcome.

One evening while I was getting ready for bed, my sergeant came and told me that the captain wanted to see me immediately. I walked into his office and saluted him, "This is Donald R. Borgman, US55164426, reporting as commanded, sir." I stood at attention. I had been in the Army long enough to understand this procedure. He responded, "At ease, soldier. I understand that you have refused to take a rifle?" I answered, "Yes sir, that is true." He said, "Soldier, do you know that I can give you a direct order to take a rifle, and if you refuse that I can place you in prison?" I handed him one of my cards that identified me as a CO and answered: "Yes sir, I know that, and if that is what it takes, I am ready. Let's go!" I already gave one of these cards to the officers when I was tried and questioned earlier. Fortunately, I had two of them. The pressure felt extreme, because I was just out of high school and very uncomfortable speaking with anyone in authority. He eventually released me to go back to my barracks.

The pressure of intimidation was incredibly uncomfortable and left me shaken for a while. Yet, this too was preparing me. Much greater pressures were in my future and I had to keep myself together and stick to simple principles and truths. This was just another step in the escalation of my war experience. Soon after these incidents, arrangements were made for another soldier and me to travel by train to Fort Meade, MD for medical training.

But I'm getting ahead of myself again. I would like to add more memories from my Fort Leonard Wood infantry basic training before moving on. A person hardly knows what to expect when they begin infantry training. We learned what a soldier had to actually do in combat to carry out orders and protect himself as well as the soldier next to him. In my case, I stayed with my company of soldiers throughout all the training activities, but maintained my CO status.

Soldiers were trained how to use the following weapons: the M1 Garand .30-06 rifle, the pistol, the Browning Automatic Rifle (BAR) .30 caliber machine gun (a weapon that could be fired from the hip or shoulder, or from a bipod), and the hand grenade. Even though I was in this training without a weapon, I followed all directions and learned how to use each of the weapons.

Most of this training was done on the rifle range in preparation for a wide variety of battlefield situations. Our training included crawling under live ammunition being fired over us. It put new meaning into the phrase: "Keep your head down!" The boys with their rifles found it very difficult to crawl that way. I also participated in this training without a rifle.

On days we marched to the rifle range, I was often assigned to road-block duty. I stopped all vehicles and individuals from entering the rifle range area. It was never a difficult duty because once the drivers heard the noise of the artillery, they were eager to turn around. I probably knew more about using a rifle than some of the boys from the city. From my youth, my father and I had hunted small game together. He taught me gun safety and had given me a small caliber rifle and shotgun. However, I neither fired a gun while in military training nor during the Korean War.

They told us it was a 20 mile march out to the range. I am not sure if that was accurate because we had no way to actually measure the distance. However, we did get up at 4:00am to begin our long march. I was often assigned to carry a litter (military name for a stretcher) because I was the only one without a rifle. Of course, I had my broom stick and toilet paper with me at all times. (You know, one can never be too prepared!) The litter was always taken on marches in case someone was injured.

I remember one occasion coming back from the rifle range. I was at the rear of my company of soldiers with my broomstick and stretcher. An officer driving a jeep approached from the rear. He stopped and asked if he could carry the litter for me on his jeep. Seeing he was a military officer I quickly obeyed. Upon arriving back at camp, I found myself in deep trouble because I returned without my litter. After my thrashing-out which consisted of small vocabulary and big profanity, I was told I would need to pay for the stretcher. But, I never heard anymore about it after that day, and I never paid for it. Such is army life.

Often I was the assigned barracks sergeant, meaning I stayed back from training activities to guard the barracks. Each compound consisted of many barracks, and we never left ours unattended.

Alone for the day, the guard sergeant represented their unit of soldiers when the captain passed through for the daily inspection. The soldier in charge is expected to salute the captain and report by name, rank and serial number. The captain typically responded with, "At ease, soldier," and we followed him through the building. If he found a bed not made correctly or any unclean condition, we were in deep trouble.

Every situation brought an experience that taught me how to be a successful and effective soldier. Even without a rifle, infantry training was very important. It helped prepare me for Korea, and it contributed to returning home as a combat medic and Korean War survivor. Infantry training became a vital component of preparation for the frontline and surviving live combat. I am thankful for it.

Chapter 6
Medical Basic Training

Immediately after completing basic training at Fort Leonard Wood, MO, I was ordered to report to Fort Mead, MD. The Military issued me a train ticket and Fort Leonard Wood was soon behind me. The train rumbled along uneventfully and I had time to collect my thoughts from experiences during basic training. Another soldier, a CO, traveled with me. Finally, I had a little time with someone who better understood the standard a CO was trying to uphold. I never saw him again after we registered at Fort Mead training camp, but it was helpful to talk with someone in a similar situation.

Upon arrival at Fort Mead, I was ordered to go to the dispensary for shots. As I left the exam room, the medic saw my scar from a previous smallpox shot. He said, "You did not need any of these shots today because you had them all before." All I could do at that point was say, "Thank you." I literally got a double shot from training. I wonder if that is why I was never sick in the military. So it goes in Army life. I was slowly getting accustomed to the Army way, "Hurry up and wait."

Fort Mead also provided basic training along with medical training, but I was the only one in the ranks who had already been through basic training. Many training exercises were similar to instruction I received at Fort Leonard Wood. Because of my prior training, I already knew how to march and do calisthenics. I understood bivouac, orders, taps, and knew how to stand at attention. Saluting an officer, dressing in a class "A" uniform, performing kitchen police (KP) duty, falling-out at the sound of the sergeant, preparing for inspection on Saturday morning, and using a pup tent were all familiar to me. There was also more time spent on the rifle range, but without the fuss about my CO classification. Rifle training was the same as it was at Fort Leonard Wood, including crawling under live bullets. I did it here again, too.

I am on the left peeling potatoes with soldiers at Fort Mead
(family photo)

Harassment of COs did not occur at this camp like Fort Leonard Wood. Rather, our classification was better understood. Several of the CO soldiers were part of the Seventh Day Adventist faith. While we did not share the same faith, the camaraderie with other 1AO classified soldiers was helpful. The fact that officers did not harass us was especially appreciated. It was a relief to be away from all the prior pressures of Fort Leonard Wood, and in particular the sergeant, our platoon leader.

Racial integration was another difference at Fort Mead. At Fort Leonard Wood, black soldiers were separated from white soldiers and everything was performed in segregated groups. The Military's racial policies were changing in response to a variety of factors and historical events. An educational site, Digital History, provides a nice summary of military racial integration.

In February 1948, President Harry S. Truman directed the U.S. armed forces to desegregate as quickly as possible. In July, he issued Executive Order 9981 calling on the military to end racial discrimination. It would take several years - and another war - before the military actually ended segregation. Three factors would ultimately lead to integration: the growing recognition that segregation undercut the United States' moral stature during the Cold War; the need to reduce racial tensions within the military; and the manpower needs produced by the Korean war.

It was the Korean War that finally led to the desegregation of previously all-white combat units. After six months of fighting, insufficient white replacement troops were available and black enlistments were high. In February 1951, the Chamberlin board was asked to reexamine its conclusions. Although it acknowledged that integrated units had fewer racial tensions than a combination of segregated units, it continued to call for a 10 percent Army quota of African Americans. At this time, 98 percent of the Army's black soldiers served in segregated units. In May, General Matthew Ridgway requested permission to desegregate his command.

In March, 1951, the Army asked Johns Hopkins University's Operations Research Office to analyze the impact of integrating its forces. Extensive surveys of troops and analysis of combat performance in Korea revealed that:

- *Integration raised the morale of African American soldiers and did not reduce that of white soldiers;*
- *Integration was favored by black soldiers and was not opposed by most white soldiers;*
- *Experience in integrated units increased white support for integration;*
- *Integration improved fighting effectiveness.*

An essential finding is that integration reduced racial tensions within the military. In December 1951 the Chief of Staff ordered all Army commands to desegregate. (Digital History, para. 7)

We all trained, ate, slept and marched together. The change spurred some racial tensions and a few serious situations where fights broke out and injuries were sustained. Fortunately, racial fights were the exception and integration went as well as could be expected for this time in history. Training kept everyone busy which seemed to be the best remedy.

Almost everything else, including guarding the barracks and barrack inspections, was the same as it was at Fort Leonard Wood. Those of us who were classified as COs were often assigned guard duty because we were looked down upon as the weak ones. At times we were not even considered true soldiers. However, our status changed on the battlefield under enemy fire. Many times the medic was the most valuable soldier on the field, especially when a wounded man needed to be evacuated. Then even the riflemen helped us.

Looking back I can see that learning to work and live together in a stressful situation was an important part of military training. Many soldiers were harassed by other soldiers for a variety of reasons. It was usually focused on conformity and often began as a form of humor. The situation would escalate fairly dramatically before lessons were learned and the harassment subsided. One such circumstance happened to a young soldier named Jesse. He was not very friendly and always seemed discouraged about military rules and regulations. Perhaps he was just discouraged about life in general. Jesse did not communicate and I never visited with him. The poor boy would not even look up at the face of the rest of us. Worst of all, he never used the showers. Understandably, no one wished to be close to him, especially considering the long hours of marching and training from four in the morning until late at night.

One evening before "lights out" was sounded, the other soldiers decided that Jesse was going to get in the shower. I watched the entire thing happen. They turned on the water, regulated the correct temperature and then asked poor Jesse to use it. He said, "No way," and resisted in every way he could. So Jesse was carried into the shower, clothes and all. He fought with all his power, but he was no match for the group of soldiers. I do not know why he did not turn off the water. But I can guess the other soldiers made it impossible to reach the valves. While in the shower, poor Jesse began to pray out loud. I soon left and returned to my bed.

One of the boys who participated with the harassment came to me where I was sitting on my bed, and I could see he was very upset. It was obvious that he was disappointed that he had participated. He said, "I feel so bad that I joined that situation with Jesse." He said more about Jesse praying to his god, and I wondered if this other soldier had ever heard anyone ever pray before. Then he said, "I will never do anything like this again." Well, this issue passed, and both this soldier and Jesse "survived."

With my Camp Mead company (military photo)

Soon we began medical basic training which was very interesting. We started out with bedside manners and duties. Our basic training paralleled initial nurse's training. Included were procedures to change sheets, help a patient in and out of bed, feeding a handicap patient, helping with dressing and undressing, walking a patient to build their strength, and many other duties that are shared with the nurses. Basic care instructions were helpful for everyone who had a role in medical care, including the soldiers who later were sent to hospitals within the United States. There were many steps and stages between being wounded in the battlefield and being able to join civilian life in the US again. A wounded soldier received first aid from a combat medic in the field and was evacuated to a nearby aid station. After stabilizing as much as possible at the aid station, the soldier was further evacuated to a field hospital in Korea for emergency treatment. When they could survive the flight, soldiers were sent to Japan where they received additional medical care allowing them to safely make the trip home to the good old USA. Once back in the US, their medical care continued.

Our training included specific instruction for a combat medic who stays with wounded soldiers in the battlefield and evacuates them to an aid station for further stabilization and care. We had to learn how to administer shots. Of course, all training requires practice, so we practiced on each other until we were able to do it correctly. We wanted everyone to learn this quickly!

I graduated from this training with a military number of 3666 declaring me a combat medic. We were issued a book titled, *The New Medic,* that further reinforced some of the combat medic duties we learned.

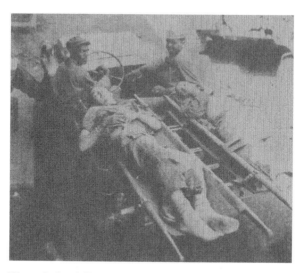

Wounded soldier on stretcher on a jeep (Song, p. 15)

This picture shows how we were trained to place a wounded soldier on a litter and take him to a waiting KD ambulance ("knock down," the ambulance could be partially collapsed for compact shipping). However, because of the rough mountainous terrain where I was stationed in Korea on the frontline, I could not use a jeep or a KD. Instead, I carried the wounded soldiers on my back over the mountain on foot.

Training to carry a wounded soldier (The New Medic, p. 27)

Easy does it.

Secure him to the litter . . .

Carry him to the proper ambulance . . .

For evacuation and further medical treatment.

Medical evacuation training (The New Medic, p. 35)

Treating an injured soldier in the field was one of the first things we learned. The order of operation was important:

 # 1   Give him a shot of morphine
This was very important and wise. It not only reduced the soldier's pain, but it also reduced the possibility of his cries alerting enemy fire of the wounded soldier's location.

 # 2   Stop the bleeding
Speed is the key! We didn't want him to bleed to death before we got him to the doctor.

 # 3   Evacuate
Speed is the key! We needed to remove him as quickly as possible for his own safety and to reduce the risk of being captured by the enemy.

Combat medics learned quickly how to solve problems and keep situations from getting worse. We learned to use every resource available. Many times this was done under enemy fire. A key factor was fast evacuation. It was very important to stabilize injured soldiers and then evacuate them quickly and quietly. The sooner a wounded soldier was treated by a doctor the better his chances were for survival. This also minimized the distraction for the other soldiers who needed to stay alert for enemy threats. Often the critically important tool was the tourniquet. It is not miraculous technology that saves lives on the battlefield. Short-term use of a tourniquet saved many soldiers who otherwise would have bled to death. When a tourniquet could not be used, we were trained to apply pressure with our hands and fingers on the vain proximal to the injury. Invaluable combat medic training sustained me during difficult situations in Korea.

Chapter 7
The Jumping Off Point

Looking back, my time at Fort Mead seemed relatively short. The training was a much better experience than my prior basic training at Fort Leonard Wood. The pressures were different and the harassment not as intense. Occasionally we were free to leave camp for several hours on Sunday. This allowed me to go to some of our Sunday morning fellowship meetings. I had been given the name and address of the home where the meeting was held. I think we met at the Hawkins' home, but I don't remember for sure. However, I distinctly recall walking into the room for the meeting and seeing another soldier. I learned during introductions after the meeting that he was Virgil Grillo from Tonasket, WA. The folks in the home invited Virgil and me to stay for lunch. Subsequently, Virgil and I had many visits and meetings together. We also took a trip to New York City and Washington, DC.

My father and mother brought my car to Maryland so Virgil and I had wheels. We spent most of our free time together. On weekends we were free to travel and often attended fellowship and gospel meetings. We enjoyed these times until he was sent to Korea. He was ahead of me in training and he left for Korea before me.

My mother, me and my dad at Fort Mead (family photo)

One evening in the barracks while walking to my bed, I saw a soldier reading his Bible. I went to his bed to visit with him because I suspected he might be a person of my faith. His name was David Wahtly, from Louisiana. I do not recall how I began the visit, but we soon discovered our common faith. So, now three of us traveled together to the Sunday morning fellowship meeting at the Hawkins' home until Virgil was deployed to Korea. David's mother, who I never met, wrote to me throughout my time in Korea and I appreciated her letters.

I eventually graduated from medical infantry training with a recognized combat medic status. Departing from Fort Mead, I was allowed a few days travel en route to Camp Stoneman, CA where we would board a ship and sail to Korea via Japan. This travel included time to visit my parents.

I drove my car from Maryland to my parent's home in Illinois. A set of twins asked for a ride. They graduated from medical training with me and were returning home at the same time. I was happy for their company and they helped me with gas money. We placed our duffel bags on each front fender of my 1948 Chevy and headed down the road. Their family met us en route where we said our goodbyes. I never heard from them again.

My time at home with mother and dad was quiet and pleasant; at least on the surface. Yet, it was evident they were filled with concern about my eminent deployment to Korea, and I was feeling anxious about all the unknowns ahead. Many soldiers were deployed to Korea and the casualties were mounting. I did not sense a feeling of hopelessness, simply a reasonably justified sense of apprehension. My short time at home was extended a little because I needed to coordinate with TWA's schedule from Chicago to San Francisco. The plane was a Lockheed L-749. Popular at the time, it was considered one of the most beautiful planes.

Lockheed L – 749 that flew me to California (family postcard)

At the San Francisco airport, I was met by a family of our faith; I believe their name was Slater. They took me to their home and later took me to Camp Stoneman. I enjoyed and appreciated their fellowship, home and help very much. Priceless connections to faith helped keep my situation in perspective.

Camp Stoneman was the San Francisco Port of Embarkation's primary troop staging center and the principal "jumping off point" for many years during World War II and the Korean War. It consisted of more than 2,500 sprawling acres filled with the sound from thousands of marching feet. Camp Stoneman sprang to life in 1942 near the town of Pittsburg, 40 miles northeast of San Francisco. Troops were received and rapidly processed for overseas service. Paperwork was completed, records updated, arrangements made for last minute training, medical and dental care were provided, and our equipment was serviced. Camp Stoneman outfitted us with everything we needed in Korea.

There is not much to tell about my time at this camp. It was a logistics stop and we were there to get supplies and be staged for Korea. We were not allowed passes to go off the base. However, one experience occurred that I will never forget in all my life. We were to be issued clothes, combat boots, and rifles before walking up the gangplank to embark the ship. We went from one warehouse to another receiving everything we would need in Korea. We came to the last warehouse when I realized that the soldiers going in the building were without a rifle. However, as they exited they all carried weapons. My CO classification anxieties immediately resurfaced when it was clear that this was where the rifles were distributed to soldiers going to Korea.

I faced and fought the issues of CO classification from my very first day in the armed forces. I felt like I just could not face one more time of trying to explain my classification record to military officers when no one attempted to understand my position anyway. Instead, I took note of the soldier in front of me as he entered the building. Then I walked to the other end of the building where the soldiers exited and waited for him to come out with his rifle. I fell in line behind him without a rifle. I was not worried about punishment, because the reprimand for any wrong doing or trouble in the Army was, "Go to Korea!" and I was going there anyway.

Going to the Theater

Chapter 8
En Route

Our training was complete and our personal supplies had been collected as we marched through the Camp Stoneman warehouses. Deployment to Korea was officially in process. Our column of soldiers continued marching beyond the final warehouse and toward the docks. US Naval Ship, *R. L. Howze* was moored and ready to ship us overseas. An enormous column of soldiers streamed aboard.

Deploying on US Naval Ship, R. L. Howze (military photo)

It didn't seem possible the ship could hold them all, but the soldiers disappeared into the ship like a sponge soaking up water. Every corner of the ship was filled with anxious soldiers. I felt a great sense of anticipation but not dread. A sense of youthful adventure accompanied our apprehension.

I was taken up with my new surrounding and it was time for a young farm boy to adjust again to military realities.

US Naval Ship, R. L. Howze (family postcard)

The *R. L. Howze* was soon underway. We glided through San Francisco Bay and turned westward toward the Golden Gate Bridge. Our ship gathered speed and we caught our last fleeting glimpses of the city and floated under the bridge. As we sailed out further into the open ocean, the coastline and everything familiar slipped beneath the horizon.

This was the next step in my series of escalations. I left home when I was drafted into the Army, and was now en route to a foreign country. There were so many unknowns and many new things to adjust to. I just took it one day at a time.

The ship that appeared so large at the dock somehow seemed smaller now. The ocean waves and swells grew larger and began to rock the ship. Before long we were a bunch of seasick soldiers. Now it became clear where all the soldiers went when we boarded the ship. We were packed so tightly together, there was barely room to turnaround. The vertical distance between the bunks was so short, I literally could not roll over or lay on my side in bed. The close quarters, rolling motion of the ship and growing numbers of seasick soldiers soon overwhelmed me and I joined the ranks of the violently seasick troops. I was miserable and weak for a couple days. What a way to get started.

During the time on the boat, I kept a diary in the form of a long letter to my parents.

> *Nov. 3, 1951*
>
> *My dear Ma and Dad,*
>
> *I wonder how you's are and how things are at home? I will write this letter on the boat so that I can mail it as soon as we land. I'll try and give you a little diary of my trip so far. We left the docks in Frisco at 4:00, Oct. 25. The tug boats pushed us out into the bay and we took off on our own power.*
>
> *We went under the Golden Gate bridge and in a few hours the lights from Frisco became very dim. At first I felt fine. I was out on deck taking everything in, ha. Some of the boys were getting sick, but I felt fine and didn't think I would get sick. But by eight o'clock that night there wasn't any boy on this boat that was as sick as I was. I never was so sick in all my life. I do not think so. Ha! I spent most of that night feeding the fish, Ha. All day Friday I stayed in bed and never went up on deck at all. But felt pretty good by Fri. eve.* (I wish to insert something here that I did not tell my parents. I remember very clearly that I was carried up on deck from down below by navy corpsmen, because I was too weak to walk that evening. When they got me to the sick bay on topside, there was no bed available,

so they put me on the floor beneath a bed. Then they treated me, but I do not remember how. After treatment I felt better. In a short time I was put on KP duty. I was initially uneasy with this, but I soon learned that it helped to get my mind off of all the water.) *By Sat. I felt pretty good and was on K.P. Sat., Sun., Mon.., and Tue. By Sunday I was right back in shape again. We had turkey for supper that day and I got the job of carving turkey and did I eat Ha! I really filled up on turkey and everything else too. We got about 2 hours off between each meal and didn't have to work hard on K.P. So that turned out as a good deal. I think we cut up nearly 400 turkeys that day. There's about 4,000 boys on this ship. Army, Navy, and Air Force. That takes an awful lot of food every day to feed that many. When we left that day the water was awful rough. They had just had a storm along the coast. The old ship really rolled around, I guess that is why I got so sick. Nearly every body was sick including the sailors. The ship was really a mess until they got it cleaned up again. That was one time when I was glad I was not a sailor, Ha! Then last Wed. I got a little sick again but not near so bad. We hit another storm but it did not amount to too much.*

Last Sat. (Oct. 27) we had kind of a unusual thing happen. One of the officers took sick and we had to go off of our course almost a day to meet a hospital ship going back to the states. The two ships came pretty close together and then they transferred him in a little inboard motor boat. It looked funny to see that little boat out in them waves. But I guess its all in the way they handle it.

My, oh My, but there sure is a lot of water in this world. Day after day and all you can see is water, water and more water. I will be glad when we get to land again because we are confined to such small quarters here. We haven't hardly got room to turn around and nothing to do. The bunks are so close together up and down that I do not have room to turn on my side. I go up on deck nearly all day long but there is nothing to do but sit or lay and it is nearly too crowded to lay down. Ha.

Well its 12:30 noon here, Sat. Nov. 3. And back in Baileyville it would be 7:30 in the evening, Fri. Nov 2. We crossed the international date line last Wed. night and by doing that we skipped a day. We did not have a Thus. or Nov. 1. We went to bed Wed. night and got up Friday morning. This is kind a hard to get figured out at first. Get that old globe down of the world and find that line on there. And maybe it will help you to get it figured out. This is an imaginary line drawn from one pole to the other and that's where the day begins. We have set our clocks back five times so far out here at sea. So that makes 7 hours behind central standard time. And I suppose we will have to set them back a couple of times more yet before we get to Japan. That is where we are going I'm sure. So when you get up in the morning Dad, I will be going to bed. When you get up say on Mon. morning I will be going to bed and it will be Mon. night for me. Can you get that figured out?

We met another ship last Tues. We could just see the top of it in the horizon. We have been sailing eight days now and I guess we still have two or three days to go. I will be pretty happy to see land again. I hope it does not take too long for this to get home and I hope I get some mail soon after I reach Japan. I made friends with some nice boys here on the boat, otherwise I was kinda alone at first because I had to leave all of my close buddies behind at Camp Stoneman. You sure make a lot of friends in the Army. But about the time you get acquainted with somebody you get separated. I miss Dave, I wish we could have stayed together.

I am going to send a little clipping along that I got from a paper here aboard ship. They print a paper here every day and that gives us the news. It tells us something about the ship and I thought it would be nice to keep it with the picture of the Ship.

We forgot something when I was home, remember Ma, how we were going to look on that globe of the world? You can see on there about where we have went. We came within about 500 miles of the Hawaiian Islands. They said first that we were going to stop at different places but I guess that was only a rumor. Because it looks like we are going right to Japan.

I thought that it would be cold when we got at sea, but it really has been nice weather. It's warm outside, you do not need a coat only at night and some of the boys are just in T-shirts. I suppose its getting pretty cold now in Baileyville? I saw in the paper where they had snow in the Dakotas. I talked with a sailor the other night and he said the weather in Japan was the same as in Illinois.

They have a small library on the ship, a small P.X. and coke machines. Movies on the deck every night and some musical instruments that we can sign out for and play if we want to. We got some good guitar players here, also violin, fiddle and ukulele.

I just took time out to read the paper and it said in there that we will land at Yokohama, Japan. That is not very far from Tokyo if I remember right. There are a lot of Japanese Sea Gulls flying around the boat today so we must be getting pretty close.

It seems as though we are pretty close to peace in Korea again. I sure hope they make it this time. The news we got today sounds pretty hopeful.

Well I can not think of any more to write about today so will stop now and finish this later.

Sunday, Nov. 4th. Just a few more lines today. I suppose you will think you are reading a book? Boy its really rough today, I can hardly write this. The sun is shining most of the time but the wind is blowing very hard. The waves splash up over the front of the boat and when you are up on deck you get a shower every once in a while. I have been up on deck all day but clear in the back of the boat and the back end nearly goes under too once in a while.

Just a month ago today I left home remember? That day I was riding an airplane from Chicago to Calf. And today I am riding a boat from Calf. to Japan. I wonder where I will be in a month from today. It seems more like a year since I left home instead of a month? Well they just called for chow so I guess I will go and eat.

Mon. Nov. 5, 1951. Just a few more lines to night and then I will mail this. They say we are going to get in port early today or tomorrow morning and I will really be glad too, to get out of such close quarters. They have a place on the ship here where we can mail letters and *then they will mail them for us as soon as we reach land. I am going to do that with this one and maybe you will get it quicker than if I try and find a place to mail it. I will write again as soon as I get to camp. But when you get this you will know that I got here alright. Hope this finds all well at home. No more for now.*

As always, Fritzie

The first stop was Camp Drake close to Yokohama, Japan. No one was sorry to leave the close quarters of the ship. A few soldiers were assigned to duty in Japan, but the majority were headed to Korea. Those of us who were going to Korea stood in formation to hear an officer brief us on conditions in Korea. This became my next "opportunity" to get personal attention from a sergeant. We had our duffel bags, and I also had a new suitcase from my mother. He looked at my suitcase, then looked at me right in the eyes and said, "Soldier where do you think you are going with that thing? Did you think you were going to a picnic or something like that?" He made it abundantly clear that nothing went with us except clothes, razors, toothbrushes, and if we had one, a small Bible to fit in our pocket; nothing else except rifles for those who accepted them. I appreciated my mother thinking of me; however, her considerations were not practical. Perhaps if I had been assigned to duties in Japan I could have kept it, but I was going into a combat zone. Either way it would have been an unnecessary burden, so I sent it back to my mother.

My brief glimpses of Japan were interesting. Everything was vastly different from what I knew. The few days passed quickly and soon columns of troops once again marched toward the docks. This time we boarded the *Akien Victory*, in groups that would stay together as we marched ashore at Inchon, Korea.

I used my time aboard this ship to write home again and explain a bit of what I saw in Japan.

7:30 A.M. Saturday – Nov . 10ᵀᴴ 1951
My dear Mother and Dad,

Well this morning finds me back on another boat and waiting to take off again. I think I will have time to write this yet and can mail it here on the boat. We came on the boat yesterday at about 4 o'clock. It took us about 3 hours to come here from Camp Drake. I am here in Yokohama again. The same place where we came in at from the states. We came to Yokohama on the train yesterday. And it was one of the most interesting rides I ever had. Got to see a lot of the country. I can not tell you as good as if you see it for yourself, but I will try and explain a little to you. First of all, the trains are nothing like our trains are. They are small. Narrow tracks and of course not half as modern as ours are. They go slow and stop about every two miles. (ha). I remember in school how we use to study about these people but a person can never believe it until he sees it for himself. There way of living reminded me much of the friends down in Mexico, remember? There way of dress too is similar to that of the Indians. What shoes they have are wooden shoes and most of the children are bare footed. The working men have a little better shoes. Toe-slit shoes. The women carry their children on their backs.

The country is very, very thickly populated. The houses in the country here are almost as close together as they are in a town back home. And the city's, well it is just one house on top of the other. No table or chairs. Unless it is a little table about a foot high in the middle of the room. Most houses have but one or two rooms. When the train would stop, men, women, and children came running towards it. We throw candy, crackers, pennies, and things like that out to them and were they ever happy to get it. Every foot of ground is farmed here. Mostly rice and vegetables. The woman do most the farm work I think, and they have no equipment either. Everything is done by hand. The farms here are about the size of our pasture and garden. In the bigger city's some of the people are dressed pretty good... And I would imagine that in Tokyo being the third largest city in the world, things would be pretty modern. I sure wish I could have went there. So much for Japan!

I am nearly out of writing paper and envelopes. I tried to buy some here in Japan but it seems to be pretty scarce. I could not get any. I only have four envelopes left. I will not write anybody but you until I get some more. I am going to try and get some on the boat here in the P.X. as soon as they open up.

The boat I am on this time is not quite as big as the other one was. But a much nicer boat I believe. It is called the Akien Victory. I do not know just when we will be leaving around noon I think and it will be three or four days traveling on water.

I think I told you this when I first went into the Army and it is still true now. I can get an emergency leave any time through the Red Cross. There has been a good many boys got an emergency leave from Korea and were home in 48 hours time. Just thought I would remind you of this again. Well I think I will have to close again for now and mail this.

I hope this finds all well at home, I am fine. I will soon be to my unit and settled down to a job. I will write as often as I possibly can.

As Always, Fritzie

The ship steamed southwest along Japan's east coast. We sailed past Nagasaki, one of the cities attacked with the atomic bomb during World War II. Once we were beyond Japan's southern coast we turned northwest toward the Yellow Sea; a body of water between China and Korea with Shanghai on the west side. We continued toward a staging area in the Yellow Sea west of Inchon and eventually slowed to a very unhurried pace.

We were told that this area of the Yellow Sea is known for strong under currents making it difficult for the captain to maintain a course. There were other ships anchored with their bows towards our ship. Our ship was moving sideways because of the strong current, and we were moving forward at the same time. I happened to be on deck of our ship and saw that a collision was eminent. We hit the bow of another ship with a loud crash and a sudden sideways jolt. But at the same time we still moved forward at a very slow pace. Frightened by the noise and sudden jerk of the ship, soldiers in the lower part feared we were bombed by one of the North Korean aircraft. Many came topside quickly and questioned what happened. There was no extensive damage to either ship, only minor injuries to a few soldiers who were close to the rail where the two ships collided.

The excitement of our collision soon passed and our ship moved to a waiting area. We dropped anchor and waited for nightfall and orders to join our units on Korean soil.

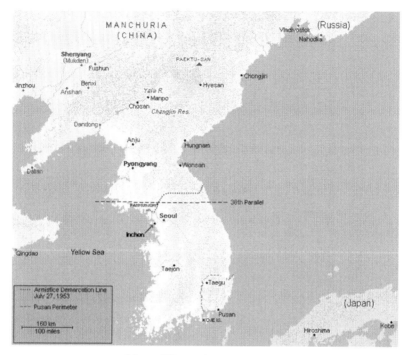

Map of Korea (Macro History)

Chapter 9
Arriving in Korea

We waited until dark before we navigated to the harbor at Inchon. The ship could not use any lights going towards the harbor because the city was under mandatory blackout conditions for safety reasons. We smelled the odors of Korea from the harbor; not a pleasant smell, and one which immediately distressed many soldiers. We quickly learned that the foul odors resulted from lack of toilets and sewer systems. These conditions were prevalent throughout Korea.

Troops prepared to unload at Inchon while it was totally dark, but I do not remember the arrival time. We were given orders to have our duffel bags packed by our beds in the lower part of the ship. We were also instructed to stand by until ordered to form a line with our designated group as assigned in Japan. Orders soon came and we assembled our groups. Slowly the line moved to the stairs and continued up onto the deck; all done orderly by command. Once I got on the deck and close to the rail I saw the landing craft down in the water. Rope ladders hung from the railing of our ship down to the smaller boats. When it was my turn to go, I went with my duffel bag over the rail, started down the rope ladder and entered the small landing craft. We stood up in the boat and were packed so tightly we could not turn around to see who was behind us. Our backpacks did not permit us to move. All was dark, not even a moon. But this was to our advantage because the enemy could not easily detect us.

The Marines had landed here earlier in the war and had pushed the North Koreans and Chinese soldiers north of the 38th parallel so we could make this landing without drawing fire from the enemy. This experience will never leave me. We were going into the war zone and did not know what to expect. Darkness gave the scene an ominous feeling.

Boarding and being brought ashore in the landing craft (Olive-Drab)

The landing craft rolled through the waves as it motored toward the shore. Tides at this location can reach as high as 35 feet. We stared into the night beyond the large steel ramp that closed us in. Soon the landing craft slowed and bumped into the shore. The ramp in front of us lowered like a castle gate over a mote and we ran ashore through the shallow water. We arrived in Korea on the Inchon shores similar to the Marines in this picture. A marching column was formed and we moved ahead single file.

Troops landing at Inchon (family postcard)

I have a clear memory of seeing many Korean people sitting all along the path we walked from the shore. This was my first time to see so many Korean people: old men, women, children and babies. The darkness and language barrier prevented communication with these people, but occasionally we got a glimpse of their faces. It was evident that they were very happy we arrived to help them fight the communists. Even in the darkness I saw enough to realize Korea was different than anything I had ever seen before in my life. The image of that night was etched into my mind and it is still clear today.

I was acutely aware of our surroundings and waves of anxious anticipation coursed through me. We had stepped into a country at war. We, as soldiers, knew there would be pain, suffering and death ahead of us. We knew somewhere in this country was an enemy whose goal was to gain possession of this land without mercy or regard for human life.

There was a very brief stay in Inchon, then I received orders to board a troop train headed to Seoul. I was on my way to my first assignment. A few other soldiers and I continued beyond Seoul until we arrived at a train stop a little to the south. A military truck picked us up and brought us further south to a hospital. It was called 121 Evacuation Hospital (121 Evac) located near a small town of Young Dung Po. Before the war, the building was a Korean school. Bombing from North Korean and Chinese forces during early stages of the war caused extensive damage to the structure. Some of the rooms did not have roofs and some windows were blown out. The Army made necessary repairs to construct an emergency room, operating room, recovery room and kitchen. This facility gave injured soldiers necessary care to stabilize them for transport to Japan on a DC-3 aircraft. In Japan, additional care was administered before their return to the United States.

121 Evacuation Hospital (family photo)

The human cost of war quickly became very real. Soldiers with a variety of injuries poured into the hospital. I came face to face with the brutality of war. In a few short weeks, I went from the land of freedom into the midst of war; an enormous transition. The contrast was so stark, one wanted to understand the reasons for war and quickly began to ask, "Why?"

Chapter 10
What Are We Fighting For?

Although I just began my service in Korea in November 1951, the war was already in progress for well over a year. There had already been advances, retreats, many casualties, and a leadership change along with many geopolitical influences affecting the war. It was complicated and confusing. Many questions could be asked when facing war, but the following two were asked almost every day at my new 121 Evac assignment:

1. "Why are we here?"
2. "What are we fighting for?"

Fellow soldiers asked many times "Why are we here in this forsaken country? There is nothing here worth fighting for!" It came up over and over: while we worked, when we ate chow and when we talked in the sleeping quarters. These questions negatively impacted our troop morale.

General MacArthur offered a domineering military style answer for the questions. "It is conclusive because the loyalty we give, and expect, precludes any slightest questioning of these orders" (Song, p.4).

General Ridgway gave strong leadership and respectful answers. Answering the first question he simply said: "We are here because of the decisions of the authorities of our respective governments." His principled respect for authority was clear and it provided overall leadership resolve.

General Ridgway felt the second question was of greater significance, and wanted every member of his command to have a full and reasoned answer.

It is not a question of this or that Korean town or village, real estate, here. It is not restricted to the issue of freedom for our South Korean Allies, whose loyalty and valor under the severest stresses of battle we recognize; though that freedom is a symbol of the wider issues, and included among them.

The real issues are whether the power of Western civilization, as God has permitted it to flower in our own beloved lands, shall defy and defeat Communism: whether the rule of men who shoot their prisoners, enslave their citizens, and deride the dignity of man, shall displace the rule of those to whom the individual and individual rights are sacred: whether we are to survive with God's hand to guide and lead us, or to perish in the dead existence of a Godless world.

If these be true, and to me they are, beyond any possibility of challenge, then this has long since ceased to be a fight for freedom for our Korean Allies alone and for their national survival. It has become, and it continues to be, a fight for our own freedom, for our own survival, in an honorable, independent national existence.

These are the things for which we fight. Never have members of any military command had a greater challenge than we, or a finer opportunity to show ourselves and our people at their best.

I would like each commander to whom it is addressed, in his own chosen ways of leadership, to convey the foregoing to every single member of his command at the earliest practicable moment (Song, p. 4).

General Matthew Ridgway (Song, p. 4)

For General Ridgway, it was no longer a fight for South Korean liberty as much as it was a crusade for the whole free world. His perspective was well founded. By the time I arrived in November 1951, many circumstances already revealed that the war to keep South Korea free was also a larger struggle between communism and the western free world. Early in the war, United Nation forces had pushed North Korean forces back from their attack on Seoul deep into North Korean territory. United Nation forces also occupied most of North Korea by early November 1950 and approached the Yalu River. In late November 1950 the Chinese joined the war and forced a substantial retreat.

I understand at one time Chinese soldiers came down by the hundreds and thousands from China across the ice on the Yalu River. In 2003, I visited with a veteran who was at the river and participated in the battle. At 16, he lied about his age and entered the Marines. He soon found himself with a rifle fighting the enemy in Korea where he was able to change his M1 .30-06 bolt action rifle to an automatic rifle. I heard of other soldiers doing this to receive more fighting power. He told me about the enemy streaming across a frozen Yalu river where he and his fellow soldiers were deployed to try and stop the advance, but the numbers simply overwhelmed them. The Chinese had a different strategy for advancing in combat where the lead soldier was the only one with a weapon. After the lead soldier was killed, the one behind him grabed the weapon and the lineup continued indefinitely.

Stories of the Chinese joining the war are told by many Korean War veterans. For instance, a story from one of my building suppliers. He served in North Korea when the Chinese joined the war, and he told what he experienced when the Chinese came down off of the ice. It is a harrowing tale that includes getting separated from his company. Searching in the dark to get back to his company exhausted him, and he reached a point where he was not thinking clearly. He found a damaged building and went in to lie down and rest. During the night he woke up and heard footsteps outside, but because of exhaustion he did not leave the building. In the morning it became obvious it was Chinese soldiers he had heard marching across the river ice and into Korea throughout the night. The enemy was now lurking and he had to sneak around in broad daylight. He finally found his company of soldiers, but not without traumatic and lasting effects. I may be the only person that knows his story, because he, like so many veterans, had a very difficult time talking about war experiences. His speech was broken and he feels very fortunate to be back in the

United States alive and without being tortured. Soldiers who fought the Chinese in North Korea were overwhelmed by the sheer numbers of soldiers advancing toward them; a situation both terrifying and deadly.

By January 1951, the Chinese and North Koreans struck again and moved below the 38th parallel. By February 1951, the Chinese and North Koreans had pushed well south of Seoul. However, the Chinese could not remain fighting south of Seoul because they outran their supply line. By March 1951, Seoul was recaptured by United Nation forces. The city of Seoul was devastated by the four changes of power within a year. From July 1951 to the end of the war (armistice and cease fire) in July 1953, there was very little territorial change. The line between North and South Korea remained roughly along the 38th parallel.

Meanwhile, there was a serious and growing conflict within the United States leadership. On several key diplomatic and strategic points, General MacArthur and President Truman were in conflict. On April 11, General MacArthur was removed from command for insubordination and replaced by General Ridgeway. The United States Constitution stipulates that military commanders will be subordinate to civilian leadership. President Truman felt that General MacArthur was usurping his authority to make foreign policy. It is interesting to note that by this time, General MacArthur had not been back to the continental United States for 11 years. He was a national hero, but his perspectives were getting increasingly out of synch with emerging national realities, and he was becoming a maverick in the field.

We were grateful for General MacArthur, but we understand that the rule of law must prevail for the privilege of freedom to exist. I have always been in agreement with one of his statements, "There is no substitute for victory!" From what we understood at the time, there was a divided command. I was told that General MacArthur wanted more troops, equipment and everything necessary to take the soldiers across the Yalu River and up into China. President Truman's advisors in the Pentagon did not agree with his request because if the United States did this, there was a possibility that Russia could join forces with China. With the United States still celebrating the victory of World War II, we did not have the resources to stand up against China and Russia.

I believe what happened with General MacArthur was the right thing. There is no room for divided command, and this disagreement represented division. War's very object is victory; not prolonged indecision. It took me some time to understand the issue, but once understood, I was in agreement. A military commander operating out of synch with the civilian government is a very dangerous situation. Following the rule of law in our Constitution, and balancing the military and geopolitical aspects of the war led to South Korea's freedom.

General MacArthur (family postcard)

Chapter 11
My First Assignment

We slept in small military barracks that had been set up near 121 Evac. Our beds were assigned to us and nearby buildings had other facilities for us including a mess hall. We were inside a fenced compound with only one gate to enter and exit. Soldiers guarded the entrance 24 hours a day. We could obtain a pass from the captain's office to go to the Post Exchange (PX) in the small nearby town. During time off from our obligations, we could walk the countryside if we wished. I did more of this later when I was better acquainted with conditions.

Hut I slept in while at 121 Evacuation Hospital (family photo)

Those of us who just arrived were given assigned duties within the hospital. I was responsible for maintaining the small stoves used in our sleeping quarters and every other room of the hospital.

There were about eight or ten of us that arrived together from the United States. One soldier in particular did not seem to understand the situation very well. While the sergeant was explaining our responsibilities and what was required at the hospital, the soldier asked "What days do I get to have off here?" The sergeant answered, "Soldier, these boys here with wounds from the battlefield need help every day." Next, the soldier asked if he could have off every Sunday. The reply was, "These boys are suffering and hurting just as much on Sunday as any other day of the week. So your responsibility is everyday!" I do not think the soldier was able for much and don't remember seeing him again.

I was responsible for maintenance in every building on the premises. With winter setting in, my workload increased, and the United States Army employed local Koreans to help me. I appreciated the additional help, because these local Korean were so hardworking. I soon recognized that these people were more thankful for Americans than words can explain. I loved them and they loved us. I even learned a few words in Korean while they learned some English.

There was one Korean man in particular who we called Sam. It was much easier for us to say "Sam" than his full Korean name. He did not know much English and I did not know Korean, but somehow we became good friends. He was not one of the young boys who worked for me. Sam was a little older and had a family; a wife and a young daughter. Sam took my clothes home with him, and his wife washed them for me. When I paid them for it, they were so happy for the extra income. They lost so much from the war's destruction; I do not know how to explain it all.

Sometimes it was my duty to guard the big gate at the compound entrance. Guards at the gate were required to search all Korean employees as they returned home in the evening. We were to look for anything they might try to take from the hospital or any of the sleeping areas. We felt so sorry for them. Even their rice paddies were destroyed by the bombs. These poor people; they had very little food and hardly anything to live on. When Sam came through the gate I searched him and felt oranges in his clothes. But I could not remove them knowing his little girl was hungry. For Sam, stealing food was not a crime. Rather, it was survival. The war stripped these people of everything they had, and there wasn't anything they could do about it. Young mothers came to me with open hands and a sad look begging for a little food to give the baby on their backs. I never refused them and gave them part of my dinner. I even saw them eat dog meat and sparrows.

I was not in Korea very long before I saw a serious casualty. Maintenance duties allowed me to access the surgical room and morgue where I have my first memory of seeing a soldier who had been killed in action. I observed the autopsy and was filled with a new sense of solemn respect as I witnessed the effects of a brutal war. From his nose to the back of his head, half the soldier's skull was missing. One night, I also watched two other doctors remove shrapnel from the top of another soldier's head. The gravity of war was now very real. We all knew there would be war casualties, but actually observing fallen soldiers brought a deeper understanding of the human cost. I was soon assigned to a place where I would begin using my combat medic training.

Chapter 12
Medical Evacuations

Medical evacuations consisted of many steps and several stops along the way. On the frontline, care began with combat medics who gave wounded soldiers necessary help, administered first aid and carried soldiers to a nearby aid station. Additional help was provided by a doctor at the aid station before the patient was transferred to 121 Evac where more medical help was available. Doctors at 121 Evac removed more shrapnel, set broken bones and many more procedures; too many to mention here. The patients were usually carried away from the aid station near the frontline using a transport vehicle or helicopter.

Helicopter used for transporting patients (family photo)

Helicopters played a critical role for medical evacuation in Korea. This was the first time in history that helicopters were used in warfare. Only one pilot could fit inside the bubble. The patient on a stretcher was placed on the exterior with room for one wounded soldier on each side. After the stretcher was secured to the helicopter framework, a heavy lid covered the patient preventing the rotor's wind from blowing directly on the soldier. Helicopters improved evacuation efforts from the frontline not only because of speed, but also because they could reach areas not passable by a jeep or ambulance.

No praise is too high for the honorable American helicopter pilots and crewmen who were committed to snatch downed allied airmen while under enemy fire. Their missions were often deep into hostile territory or sometimes even out at sea. About a month before I arrived in Korea, there was an incredible rescue mission performed by helicopter pilots. Five Fireflies, British aircraft deployed from a ship, were scheduled to bomb a railway tunnel well behind enemy lines in North Korea. The Fireflies easily found their target, but one of the British aircraft was hit by ground fire. Its pilot made a creditable crash landing in a rice paddy, and an American rescue helicopter was called in. While waiting for the recue team, remaining Fireflies circled protectively above the downed pilot who was observed calmly collecting gear and personal weapons before leaving the aircraft. We knew the North Koreans and Chinese were ordered to fire at the cockpits of any of our downed aircraft prohibiting communication with our downed pilots. With the enemy less than 25 yards away and under heavy fire, the American helicopter landed alongside the downed airmen. Upon landing, American helicopter crewmen leapt out of the helicopter while continually shooting. They held off the enemy while they rescued the pilot and lifted off. The Korean War saw many of these rescue missions where helicopter pilots and crewmen saved many from death and captivity.

My first involvement in medical evacuations began during my assignment at 121 Evac. The Army found out I drove a large semi truck in civilian life. It was decided that I would be reassigned from building maintenance to transporting injured soldiers. In Korea, the military had two different kinds of vehicles for medical transport: the smaller of the two was called a KD, and the other was a converted bus.

KD vehicles used for transporting patients (family photo)

I was issued a military license to drive both types of vehicles, and I began my new assignment transporting injured soldiers primarily in a medical transport bus. The bus had all seats removed and was redesigned to permit patients on litters to be placed along the sides of the bus. My newly assigned duties better aligned with my medical training. I was directly involved in providing medical care for the remainder of my time in Korea. Interestingly, the license I was issued in Korea helped me after returning home. My truck license had expired while I was in Korea and I needed to apply for a new one. The licensing office asked to see my present license so I gave them the military license issued in

Korea. They looked at it and quickly said, "With that rating, you do not need a test!"

Driving medical transport vehicles was interesting and we always had to be ready. When a helicopter was on approach to 121 Evac with an injured soldier, the sergeant yelled, "Chopper coming." We knew such announcements meant to get down to the landing pad, remove the injured soldier from the aircraft and get him up the hill to the emergency room. A KD vehicle facilitated the transport by getting help as soon as possible; especially when the weather was bad. These arrivals made for some exciting moments.

Transferring patients from incoming helicopters to the emergency room did not take much of my time. Usually I spent my time transporting patients with the converted bus from 121 Evac to an airstrip where they were flown out of Korea.

The bus was designed with two mounted brackets for each litter along the sides of the vehicle, and two straps per litter came down from the top of the vehicle. The litter attached to the metal side brackets, and was secured with two straps from the top. The straps are visible in the next picture of another soldier and me. I used this ambulance almost every day to transport patients.

There were two rows, an upper and a lower, on each side of the vehicle. When fully loaded I could transport twelve patients from 121 Evac to the airstrip built near the Han River by Army engineers for this purpose.

Another soldier and me by a bus ambulance I drove (family photo)

DC-3s were used as medical transport planes and flew patients to Japan for further treatment. These planes were converted by removing the seats and installing brackets and straps similar to the inside of the bus ambulance. This plane is sometimes referred to as a Douglas C–47B. I backed the ambulance to the rear door of the plane and transferred the patients from my vehicle into the aircraft.

DC-3 similar to the one used to transport patients from Korea to Japan (Song, p. 27)

I transported patients to the airstrip nearly every morning. Sergeant Evans had responsibility for emergency medical care. He arranged the time for me to bring my vehicle up to the emergency room door where the patients could be brought and loaded into my vehicle. I was responsible for safe transfer to the airstrip by the Han River.

Once I had all the patients in the bus and as comfortable as possible, I drove through the guard gate and toward the airport. I was very careful not to make quick turns, hit any bumps, and most importantly, I remembered to talk to the soldiers. At this point, communication was very important; they needed to be reminded they were on their way out of Korea. Most were very happy and their pain was manageable. They were going home to good old USA via Japan and then to a hospital in the States. As I arrived at the airstrip, I backed up to the door on the left side and behind the wing of the aircraft.

The door of the aircraft was usually open with a nurse waiting to receive patients. I had help from other soldiers at this airstrip transferring patients into the aircraft, and making sure each part of the stretcher was secure in its proper place. When all patients were loaded on the aircraft, the nurse was busy making sure each soldier was comfortable. I sometimes stayed in the aircraft and helped her. The two pilots had the engines running and were ready to leave as soon as the nurse and I had patients quieted down and comfortable. I jumped out of the plane, closed the door and the nurse locked it from the inside. I drove my vehicle away and the pilots began taxiing to the runway on their way to Japan.

By mid-morning, I usually finished my airstrip transport obligation for that day. I often went into the barracks at the airstrip before going back to 121 Evac. Nurses at the barracks often had a hot doughnut for me. I loved my responsibilities of helping these people. We were on duty seven days a week and as can be imagined, I saw most every kind of injury that existed, I felt that my efforts helped those in great pain, and it gave me satisfaction that they were on their way back to the United States.

When I wasn't transporting patients to the airport, I often transferred soldiers to other hospitals. I was also responsible for the basic maintenance of the ambulance. I kept it full of gas, changed the oil and made sure it was clean and in good running order. Even when I was not immediately busy with an assignment, I had to be nearby and available for emergency trips.

Chapter 13
Life at 121 Evacuation Hospital

Below is a picture of some of the soldiers I worked with at 121 Evac. It was taken on the steps going into the building where injured soldiers received treatment. Unfortunately, I don't remember any of their names. These soldiers likely received similar training at either Fort Mead or Fort Sam. In the photo, I see my rank of private first class. I entered the Army with the rank of private. During my time at 121 Evac, I was promoted to private first class, the same rank with which I was discharged. I was not in the Army for rank because it does not take rank to help a wounded soldier.

I'm on the bottom stair in the center at 121 Evac (family photo)

Below are pictures of a few of the other transport activities. The large helicopter was not used for evacuation of injured troops from the frontlines. Rather, it was used for transporting supplies and personnel from one area to another. Both pictures show a portion of the 121 Evac building in the background. The patient in the lower photo may have been a Korean soldier being transferred to a Korean Hospital.

Large helicopter landing in front of 121 Evac (family photos)

There are several anecdotal stories that help provide a picture of what life was like. 121 Evac had air raid warnings called "Bedcheck Charlie" when enemy aircraft were identified flying in air space near the hospital. The term "Bedcheck Charlie" originated from earlier wars where a small Russian bi-plane flew at night looking for lights and targets to drop its load of small bombs. A loud siren activated when enemy aircraft neared 121 Evac. We were instructed to put out all lights, report to our assigned stations and stay there until further notice. We were all trained to follow procedures in the event of an actual bombing.

When my duties changed from building maintenance to patient transport, my orders also changed during the air raid warnings. At the sound of the siren, I reported to my vehicle and prepared to move patients to a different location should we actually be attacked. I waited until the siren sounded again to alert us that the enemy aircraft were no longer a threat. Sometimes warnings sounded more than once in a night, in which case I often stayed and slept in my vehicle for the rest of the night. But fortunately, we never had an actual raid during the time of my duties at 121 Evac.

Nurses did a great job assisting with the recovery of injured patients. I believe when a nurse walked into a room of a soldier in the morning after he was wounded in action, and she greeted him with, "Good morning, soldier. How are you this morning?" the sound of a female voice did more than pills.

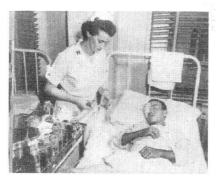

US nurse changing a Korean soldier's bandage (Song, p. 15)

I got to know most of the nurses pretty well. Sometimes they needed a little help with maintenance, like maybe the heating stove went out and required cleaning in their sleeping quarters. One day they asked a very special favor of me because I had a vehicle for transporting patients.

They wanted me to take them with the ambulance to a hill early some morning so they could watch the sun come up. I had no idea if they were associating this with sunrise service or not. This request was not in the line-of-duty.

I did not answer them immediately. My first silent response to myself was, "No way." If I was questioned about this, I really did not have a legitimate story. I felt if I did this I would be totally out of line. But I also knew the punishment was, "Go to Korea," and I was already there.

As I contemplated the request, I realized these nurses were far away from home and did not have opportunity to see much more than the inside of the hospital where they saw the same things every day; more blood and wounds of all different nature. Maybe it was the first time for some of them to be away from home. I had a change of thought. These nurses needed something different to see. I needed a plan.

First, I needed to find a hill, and second, it needed to be a hill where I could get my ambulance close to the top. This had to be done in the dark while waiting for the sun to rise. I found a solution and instructed the nurses to meet me at a designated time and place; near my vehicle one morning. They all knew where that was.

The guard did not even look inside as I went through the gate. I exited the gate often and the guard knew me well. He would not think of me doing anything different than transporting patients. It was a nice morning and I think all the nurses enjoyed it. No trouble ever came of this little jaunt.

On another occasion we had free time after completing our duties. I remember an afternoon in Seoul when another soldier and I decided to observe some of the war damage caused from the North Koreans when they marched into Seoul in June, 1950. We were told the capital buildings sustained extensive damage, and wanted to see for ourselves.

We parked my vehicle and began walking on the sidewalk that wrapped around the capital building; maybe 50 yards away from the building. We were looking at the damage caused by bombs, machine guns and small arms fire. Then we decided to go venture inside the building. We proceeded by turning onto one of the sidewalks that went from the street to the building. Nearby a South Korean soldier stood at attention with his rifle in his hands. He spoke to me as I went by him, but I did not understand Korean, so we could not communicate. Then we heard a noise behind us that was very familiar. The two of us stopped immediately. The noise was from the live cartridge being removed from the magazine when the soldier placed it into the chamber of his rifle. I did not need to be told what that meant. Apparently Korean guard soldiers were given orders forbidding anyone to enter that building. We immediately stopped and went back to our vehicle.

Back at 121 Evac, every soldier needed to perform guard duty. I did my obligation without a weapon because I was a CO. When it was dark, we walked the fence all the way around the compound. The threat of fires was possibly the most important reason for constant watch. At least once each night the sergeant advanced towards us from the front and we said with a loud voice, "Who goes there?" Then he identified himself as sergeant of the guard.

It was easy to get caught up in all the military activity and lose our overall life perspective. Occasionally in the evening, United States newsreels were shown in one of the rooms at 121 Evac. This confirmed our confidence in the good old USA. Sometimes under combat conditions when we were seeing a lot of blood and death, the human mind had difficulty processing it all. In addition, propaganda from the enemy would have liked for us to believe that the United States was also being destroyed while we were fighting for Korea. I believe the movies provided evidence that the good old USA was as we remembered it.

121 Evac filled a vitally important role for wounded soldiers, but did not receive much attention or recognition. Military operations were vast and complex where each part needed to simply function efficiently and effectively regardless of its visibility. However, one day President Syngman Rhee, of Korea, visited 121 Evac. I saw him that day; he is on the left.

Left - President Of South Korea Syngman Rhee,
Center - General Matthew Ridgeway (Song, p. 3)

Korean Experience Beyond Duties

Chapter 14
Life for the Koreans

Military life in Korea was quite different from the life of the South Koreans. In the military, vehicles and aircraft transported supplies, equipment and people in and around the country. Meals were provided and everyone was working hard at their assigned duties. Outside the military operations the South Koreans lived a substantially different and difficult life. I witnessed sobering poverty and hardship. A nearby Korean farming village bore no resemblance to the Illinois farming community where I was raised. War completely disrupted their lives, and for some, even the next meal was in question. The snapshots below show a view of the Korean landscape outside the 121 Evac compound. These scenes made deep impressions on an 18 year-old farm boy experiencing a war torn and underdeveloped country.

Korean farming village (family photo)

Countryside of Korea (family photos)

Korea did not have many roads at the time. With the exception of the military, there were no cars or trucks. Cities had a few buses, but no bus service extended out to the countryside. The United States Military built some roads as quickly as possible which supported wartime operations. Koreans traveled by foot and oxcart, but generally traveled very little.   Outside the cities, they lived with extended families in small farming villages where they tilled the ground.

Because it was underdeveloped, Korea lacked toilets and sewer systems in most areas.   Offensive odors extended throughout the countryside.   Some veterans remember smelling Korea from several miles out in the water when we arrived.   This was partly because the fields were fertilized with human waste.   Add to this the stench of old human blood and deteriorating bodies from the war and one will quickly understand the odious scent that greeted us in Korea. The smell filled the breeze and drifted for miles.

Fertilizer was carried to the fields in large buckets pulled on ox-drawn carts. A man walked along the side and guided the ox pulling the bucket full of the unimaginable.   It all seemed so primitive, but for these people basic farming methods were precious tools for survival. Korea had little or no modern farming machinery.   Much of the rural underdevelopment was due to exploitation from Japanese occupation that began in the late 19th century.   Oxen were widely used for farm work. Farming in general was highly labor intensive making it difficult for the Koreans to quickly restore war damaged fields to productive rice paddies.

Plowing with an ox, 1952 (family photo)

Rice farming near 121 Evacuation Hospital (family photo)

Farmer working field amid artillery, 1952 (Song, p. 19)

For many years, the Japanese repressed the Korean people. Now the Chinese and North Koreans bombed what little possessions they had, including their rice fields where their food was produced. As a result, no rice was harvested, people starved and widespread hunger added to Korea's miseries. Many ask if I enjoyed the rice and Korean diet during my time in Korea. But at that time, Korea was a war torn country that could not produce enough food and rice to feed its own people. Rather than being a further burden on Korean resources, soldiers were fed American rations.

Korean women planting rice, 1990 (family photo)

I took this picture when I visited Korea in 1990. It shows how rice is grown in shallow water. There is far more rice production in this picture than there was in 1951. The war so severely damaged the rice fields they could not hold the necessary water to support healthy plants. Inability to repair damage quickly led to missed growing seasons and crop failure. Additionally, most stores were destroyed by bombs. With 90% of Korea invaded by the enemy, the effects of the war drained the economy and left a country that could not support itself. Many Korean people begged food from American soldiers. They pointed to my bread and pleaded for just the crust. It was so pitiful I would give them the complete slice.

I took snapshots near 121 Evac which represented what most of Korea looked like. Often, when I was not transporting wounded soldiers, I borrowed a camera and hiked into the countryside to become more acquainted with Korean life.

Left - Rice harvest, 1952
Right - School children by a Buddhist Temple (family photos)

Koreans often bowed to me as I walked along. You can see from the pictures, children loved to walk with me. They also loved to have their picture taken. On occasion, two boys liked to hike with me up the side of a hill.

Photo of me with two Korean children (family photo)

From this vantage point, we saw a broad agricultural valley and 121 Evac in the distance; the upper right hand side of this picture. One day, these two boys wanted to show me a Buddhist Temple. They took me inside, but I forgot to remove my shoes. Removing shoes is very important in Korea. The boys pointed, spoke loudly and did not need English to make it clear that shoes were not permitted in the temple. I removed them quickly, and I felt relieved they understood I did not intend to be disrespectful.

My walks and interactions were a pleasure, and a love for these people grew inside me. This may have been one of the most important parts of my Korean War experience. The impressions and memories helped me understand that the simple decency of respectful human interaction transcends all the bluster, brutality and madness of war.

The war affected everyone in Korea and stories abounded of struggles for survival. It wasn't uncommon for children to be hidden away, then left on their own when parents were killed in the war. One story in particular includes a young girl and some younger children; probably her siblings. Though I wasn't personally involved with this experience, it illustrates conditions in Korea when families were separated by war. "Some of the family members were killed and remaining members needed to just make the best of it; whatever that consisted of. They could not speak a word of English. Some of the soldiers paid her to wash clothes. The only understandable words she said were, 'Washy, washy,' and thus became her name among the soldiers" (Hickey, p. 168). Today, I often think about people like "Washy, washy" and wonder where she is now. Her situation was typical among families torn apart and distraught, and I saw scores of people like this who represented the devastating effects of war; they left a deep impression.

Life for the Koreans

Left - Women washing clothes
Right - Women drying clothes on the river side (Song, p. 28)

The scenes above give a little picture of the desperate struggle for survival. Life was hard. People washed clothes in the river and dried them along the banks on the rocks. The women who washed my clothes worked in a scene very similar to this. They needed income, and yet there were almost no stores. Hard to understand, but the look on their faces communicated a desperate struggle of survival.

Below is the money issued by the South Korean Government during the war. At the time, the exchange rate was 6,000 Won to the US Dollar. One of these was worth 16.6 cents US.

Korean money (Paul Noll, para. 1)

The currency replaced the prewar money. The new money had a picture of Syngman Rhee, South Korea's President. A Korean man's wages were 1,000 Won a day in those days. The United States Military issued currency to soldiers so we could buy things from the civilians and hire them to do things for us.

(Olive-Drab)

Shown are Korean refugees going south soon after the war started. They sought protection from the enemy. Hickey explained the situation well in his book.

> *The day's journey southward across the open plain from Pyongyang could not be seen and forgotten. Full 50,000 souls pouring like lava across the fields. A continuous moving column stretching for thirty miles. Close to, it was a fearful spectacle. Men, women and children fleeing from the fear of death, rape and capture with all they could carry. Mothers stumbling across the ploughed paddy–fields with a baby tied behind, a baby in the womb and bedding on the head. (Hickey, p. 144)*

Stories like this help illustrate the human impact of the war I witnessed.

Chapter 15
Korean Personal Stories

In more recent years, I appreciated hearing personal firsthand accounts from a few Koreans who survived the war. Their stories are shocking, fascinating and dreadful records of Koreans escaping the communist North Korean Army. This digresses from my own personal experience, but these archives portray what I saw in Korea better than I can explain. One account was shared by Sungmi Pahk. She escaped to the city of Pusan with her parents in 1950. Sungmi is now a Korean minister who Joann and I met at a 1990 church gathering in Korea.

SUNGMI PAHK

In 1950 when the Korean War broke out we were in North Korea. A government official had taken my father's car away from him, and father knew that we needed to flee from there to the south for freedom. In early December he went to the backyard of the house and he digged a hole in the ground to put the house treasure in it. When I saw my father doing that I went into my room and packed my treasures, dolls, little toy dishes and so on, into a small suitcase. I gave it to my father. He knew that it had no value but he received it. Soon after that we left for the South. When we came to PyungYang (north Korea's capital city) to cross the river all the bridges were broken down by air-raid bombing. We had to wade through the shallowest water, which was waist deep to grownups. I was put on the top of the bedding which my father carried on an A-frame on his back so I wouldn't get wet. I saw my mom and aunties crying when their clothing become like stiff boards because it was freezing cold. We were 15 of us, Grandpa, Grandma, uncles, aunties and cousins. I was the oldest child and had two younger brothers. My youngest brother was only a few months old baby. War is such a desperate time and our own lives were in grave danger. I saw quite a few abandoned babies. It was not easy to take my eyes off them. We had two babies in our group so that was enough struggle just to keep them. Sometimes we had to hide in a cave because at times like that if a baby cries that can endanger all of our lives. When we came to a certain place, there were a few uniformed UN soldiers who kept pointing people to go in a certain direction. When our family came to them they held my youngest uncle who was only 17 years old (high school boy) and would not let him go. So my father and older uncle begged them and they finally reluctantly let him go with us. That incident gave a suspicious feeling about them to my family so we walked a short way from them and quickly turned toward the other direction and away from the crowd and went into a mountain area. Soon after that we heard terrible gunfire and heard later that most of them were killed and those soldiers were communists and disguised in UN uniform! When we got to the 38th parallel line which is the division line between South and North Korea, all the women folks felt they could not go on because their feet were swollen and bleeding. They urged the men folks to go ahead of us because when the communist soldiers come they will kill the men first. So they left us and went on about 2.5 miles but when they thought of us left behind with no man to help us they could not take any more steps away from us so they quickly came back and found we were sitting at the same place. They urged us to go and throw away most of the goods, and just carry the babies and jewels We used the jewels to trade for food because money had become useless. When we came further down we saw a freight train going down south. It was packed full of people and a lot of people were on the top of the train so 15 of us went up to the rooftop of the train and we held each others arms so none of us would slip off the sloping rooftop. It was a very, very slow trip because so many places on the rail were broken by bombing. We would travel a short distance and fix the rail so many times. It was a steam engine so when we passed through tunnels thick black smoke just about made us choke to death. Grandma covered us with a quilt when we went through a tunnel and kept calling each one of her grand children's names. When she called one of my cousins name who was 4 years old she did not answer and she realized quickly that she was suffocating and she quickly gave her first aid (mouth to mouth resuscitation) and she revived. We were 3 days on the rooftop of this train and finally arrived in Pusan City which is in the southeast corner of Korea. The whole of this trip took 35 days and all of us came safely.

Some of our current Korean ministers were very young during the war. They also described their wartime experiences. The stories are gripping accounts filled with suffering, lack of food, no place to sleep, homelessness and fear of death. Each also expressed a heartfelt gratitude for the United Nation Forces and the help that defeated the forces of tyranny making freedom possible.

Two additional accounts were shared at the 2006 Korean War Veteran's Reunion. Myong-Ku Ahn and Sun Wha Hong had the courage to tell their stories. They offer great insight into what the Koreans endured. I am glad these stories are kept alive to illustrate what happens to a country when an enemy takes away freedom.

Myong-Ku Ahn

I was, as I said it before, I was old enough to remember many of the Korean War stories and we already heard many of those stories from your point of view. I had my own way of looking at things and there are two indelible experiences I went through, and I think I'm about out of time and don't know what to say. I do not know why I wasn't dead. I had two really close occasions so I should have not been here. The first one has to do with real war stories it's not a more upbeat type. I think it might be because we have heard about the war stories, but I haven't heard much about Communists when they come in. I grew up with one of the six siblings of my parents and we lived in Myung In Dong and I know Jacobson's would probably know where that is. The 25th of June we were in Seoul, right across from Hosung in Gahng, which is Confucius Teaching Institution and sort of a sacred ground for the Koreans and that's where all the government officials learned the ethics to become – they had to pass the test to become the government official. We lived close enough and first thing they did when the Communists came in, I think the 27th or so, so they asked all their neighbors of the families and people out for a meeting. I was only thirteen years old then, and I was very curious so it was right across the street from me and I went to that beautiful place, it was full of trees and nice yard and all very well taken care of. They were having a meeting and I realized it was a people's court, they were holding. I saw there were two or three men they caught as an enemy of the people and I realized they were my father's friends. In fact, one of the things they were first did they came to my house and I am sure they came to arrest him and he knew that so he hid. My Mother said, "Go look, he's not here." I knew where he was because I was in the room that he came and opened the door and looked at me. I was a child, and asked me where he was, "where is your father?" I said, "I don't know." I knew my father hid so I'm not going to let them know, and I guess I looked innocent enough they left. They went out and didn't search any more. So he escaped with that and yes, if they caught him, he'd be one of those people there. Then after a while, there were some people gathered around outside and they read some so called crimes of those people and a few just clapped hands, I'm sure they were planted. That was enough, the man announced that they were found guilty, and thank you for finding the people guilty. They took them down and tied them against the tree and shot them, and I actually saw this. You know how Communists do and how they ruled. It was just pure terror that they planted. Because they eventually – my father was caught, they caught my father. You can hide so long because he couldn't go down south, to escape the Communist occupation. I remember one of those occasions that my life was spared. Then, of course, MacArther had the U.S. land in Incheon on September 28th, they recovered Seoul and just before the U.S. came in, there was something going on in that ground that I did mentioned -- the Confucians, the learning place. We had a big tree and I liked to climb up the tree because I could not see far enough. I was young enough so I climbed up and sure enough there was the Communist Army there in full dress, some of it was close to me. They were being pushed out of Inchon and Pusan. Then I was watching them and I heard a bullet fly through, and there was no doubt, even though I was young, it was aimed at me. So I quickly came down and I think I stayed there just a little bit, then I got down, just tried to figure out where it was coming, and a few minutes later an officer, a Communist military officer with guns came to our home. They saw me they said, "Do not you ever get up there." Course I knew I was not ready to go back up there. So that's one of those occasion I do not know why I was spared, my life was spared.

There's another occasion that my life was spared. I was too young and my sister was two years even younger and my mother did not have my father we see that without the head, you know, we hear in the Bible what happens - it flops about - and without my father around my mother was helpless. She had hoped that since they took him, they might have taken him to the north and my father originally came from the north. She decided to stay with the youngest two who could not really travel easily with her, so the rest of my brothers and sisters were sent to the south to avoid the *war, and she stayed behind. She just did not feel like she could take us with her on a trip during the war. She decided it might be safer to go to be getting out of the city and to avoid the war zone and we ended up in another town – we walked over there. The place we stayed, in fact, one day the bomb dropped, right there! This is another one of those cases where I think my life was spared. That morning, my mother woke up and told me, "I had a very strange dream. This is some omen that is not good, today. I want you to go down to the place where we were staying had a bunker because during the war and many people dug some bunkers for protection -- she said, "We may need that. You go down there and clean it up." So I went in there and was cleaning the bunker when this happened. The bomb dropped, it was napalm type and instantly the house went in flames and my sister got a superficial burn. So we were there, but my mother also got out of the house. She knew where I was, she knew I would have been safe, but my sister, she was afraid she was still in the burning house so ran right back into the house to get her, of course, she was not there. She ended up looking for her and just about all burnt up and her body was in there. Most of you served in the hospital during the war, and you know what it was like. I just entered that year in the junior high school there in first grade and started learning ABC's and I learned father and mother. I walked to the Americans who were just pushing the Communists out of the area and I mentioned my mother and did not know how to say, she was sick and so on, and there was my mother. I think there were some officer she must have noticed that and sent some people and realized there was a sick person there and they evacuated, and she had actually passed away on that evacuation train, so I lost my parents. This is what the war is about, I think. They were real experiences from my prospective. I ended up coming to the country in 1960. From then on it took me a while to find my lovely wife and took another so many years to find the Truth. Once I found the Truth, I just am so happy!! (KWVR, p. 77)*

    Sun Wha Hong
*   I just cannot tell you how thankful I am that the US soldiers, American soldiers, came to Korea when we were in such a lost estate. Our country had been under the Japanese regime occupation for thirty years and we suffered a lot because we were not allowed to use Korean language or write it. So they were going to almost have a genocide, just get rid of all the Korean people from the history books and from the earth but we still survived. There were so much shortages of things and yet we had a taste of a democracy in South Korea when North Korea was having the taste of Communism. There were a lot of struggles and it ended up in the Korean War. We were just in one word, a pathetic chaotic country, and yet our friends here the soldiers came to Korea and restored our peace and then the freedom that we hear so much. God worked in mysterious ways that He made the Japanese come over to our country, and when they left, that is when Don Garland and Sproulie Denio came, they had opportunity to come to .Korea. They started, and to make it even better, the Korean War was there. We became*

desperate people and I think all our country's people were seeking and so we were so thankful whatever Americans did. I was just a little toddler at the time of the Korean War, but I always had this warm feeling whenever I saw an American they were the saviors. The old soldier never dies, but fades away, but because of the old soldiers the Truth is there, it does not fade away, but it is just always the same and we can enjoy eternal life and I am thankful for that. (KWVR, p. 80)

I met many Korean people during the war and I instinctively knew they suffered. Yet, because of the language barrier, I did not fully appreciate their situation. I am grateful to have these stories from people who survived the war. As a soldier, I felt detached from their reality. We were in the same war, but I had the hope of going home to a better life and they seemed so drained of hope. There were vast differences in our situations, but I felt an eager desire to help in some way.

Chapter 16
Faithful Connections

South Korea's capital city, Seoul, is located south of the 38th parallel. 121 Evac was located near Young Dung Po and the Han River, both of which are south of Seoul. Two of our ministers, Sproulie Denio and Don Garland, crossed this river on June 25, 1950 en route to the airport as they escaped the country. Soon after they crossed, the bridge was bombed making evacuation from Seoul much more difficult for remaining civilians. Even though Sproulie and Don could not be in the country, they had a dedicated interest in Korea. They and other ministers put in lots of effort to stay in contact with the soldiers of our faith serving in the war.

Soon after I arrived at 121 Evac, I received a letter from Jack Carroll, an American minister. I don't know how he got my name or knew I was serving in Korea, but I certainly appreciated the letters. Somehow our ministers kept a list of us and tried to give us spiritual help with their correspondence. It was very real to me that God was guiding our ministers so that soldiers at war received fresh thoughts, spiritual bread and encouragement.

In his letter, Jack Carroll asked if I knew that there were two other soldiers who shared our faith at 121 Evac. I was shocked. I was not the only person of my faith working at the hospital. A minister on the other side of the enormous ocean helped and encouraged me. His letter told me about Ted DeWitt, from Nebraska and Kenneth Hughes, from Ohio. I found these two soldiers quickly with no problem. Both worked in the recovery unit, and stayed with the wounded until they awakened again. Sometimes they needed to stay with patients until late at night. I sat with them many times and visited during these long evenings.

At one point, I bought a guitar from a soldier. Ted and I both played guitar well enough to entertain ourselves. We weren't ready to cut an album, but it provided a brief distraction from war activities. He and I spent some of our evenings making music. Later, I sold the guitar to another soldier.

Myself, Chuck Louis, Virgil Grillo, maybe Kenneth Hughes, Ted DeWitt
(family photo)

Another soldier of our faith, Virgil Grillo who I met at Fort Mead, also served in Korea at the same time. He did not work at 121 Evac, but he also received letters from the ministers. The letters told him about us at the hospital and he came two different times to see us. Virgil was a cook at another location. He rose in the ranks quickly and reached the rank of master sergeant before leaving Korea. His rank provided him more liberty than I had as private first class.

Other soldiers who shared my faith came and went from 121 Evac. Some went to Japan for medical needs, and some were given different assignments. I appreciated the fellowship and sustaining power of our common bond.

Ted DeWitt on left - others unknown (family photo)

Left - Chuck Louis and Virgil Grillo
Right - David Wahtly (family photos)

Unknown, unknown, Arvid Klinstick, unknown (family photo)

David Wahtly, unknown, unknown, me (family photo)

Korean Soldier and Arvid Klinstick, Seoul, 1952 (family photo)

The above picture was taken in 1952 of a Korean soldier and Arvid Klinstick from Wisconsin. They are standing on a street in Seoul. Much of Seoul looked just like this during the war.

Chapter 17
Rest and Recuperation in Japan

Ted DeWitt and I spent quite a bit of time together. We decided we wanted to go to Japan together for rest and recuperation. By this time, I corresponded with Sproulie Denio and Don Garland who were in Japan. Again, these are the two ministers who were in Korea studying the language when the war started and had to leave for Japan with little more than the clothes they were wearing. However, they continued studying Korean in Osaka, Japan.

Ted and I wanted to go to Osaka to meet Sproulie and Don and personally thank them for their letters. We looked forward to much needed spiritual fellowship. Osaka was not the common destination for soldiers to get rest, recuperation and entertainment. Our request must have seemed unusual when we submitted it to the sergeant and commanding officer of 121 Evac. We feared questioning and denial. Yet, the officers granted permission and this seemed like another example of receiving heavenly help.

Having the authorized papers signed and in our hands, Ted and I went to the K12 airstrip where a DC-3 was waiting for us. We were on our way to Japan and a much needed break from the events and war activities in Korea.

I wrote my parents a letter detailing our time in Japan:

Monday Eve, Aug. 4th, 1952
Dear Ma and Dad,

Well Ted and I got back from Japan this forenoon so I must get busy and write as it is over a week ago that I wrote. I guess I better give you a little summary of our trip as you probably are anxious to hear. First of all, I will tell you that we had a very enjoyable trip. Only I was just dead tired today. I slept all afternoon. We got postponed one more day because of bad weather. So we did not leave until Tuesday last week. We left the Air Port out here at noon and got to Osaka, Japan about 4:30.PM. The Army took us out to Camp. Which is at Nara, about 35 miles from Osaka. They gave us a steak supper and our class "A" uniforms. It almost killed us to wear a tie again (ha). By ten o'clock that evening we were ready to leave and were on our own until ten o'clock last night. We slept at camp that night and got up early the next morning. Got a train and went to Osaka. You can get your map of Japan and find these towns I mention. Osaka is about the same as Chicago in size and just about as busy down town too as the loop is. So you can just about imagine Ted and I not knowing where we were going. Could not ask anybody anything, because we could not speak Japanese. We did not know if there were any workers (ministers of our faith) in Osaka or not. But we did have an address from there. We thought all of the workers were in Tokyo, which they were until a month ago. So we tried to get connection to go to Tokyo, which is about 350 miles over night ride. We even had a plane reservation. But our Army orders read Osaka area only, so we got scared out. So we gave that up. So we looked around until we found an interpreter to write this address of Sproulie Denio,. (a worker) in Japan, then we went and gave it to a taxi driver and he started off across town. After we had rode about 20 minutes we went past a Army hospital. then we wondered if any of *the saint boys were stationed there? We got our list out and sure enough Willis Stork was there. So we told the driver to turn around and let us off there and we went in and found Willis. So then we had nothing to worry about. But I never was so lost and wondering what, how and where to go in my life (ha.) You know back home you can ask questions but when you can not speak the language you really are up the stump. So that first day in Japan I will never in my life forget. (ha) But the day is not over yet: We found Willis then and what a relief that was. He knew where the workers lived. There are two in Osaka, Sproulie Denio and Don Garland. They were having an English Bible study that night for a group of young college boys and girls. So we went to that. The boys were quite surprised to see us. The Bible study was very, very interesting. Then after the Meeting the boys asked us to stay with them. So I did. Ted went back to the Hospital with Willis. I certainly enjoyed that night. The boys have a house rented, I slept on the floor as is the old Japanese custom any way (ha). This all happened in one day. The next day: Ted and Willis came over and the five of us had dinner together. First Sproulie and I went down town together. Then in the afternoon Don, Ted, Willis, and I went down town and shopped around in some of the great Japanese department stores.*

These two workers stayed in Seoul and of course were anxious to hear about it as I am getting to know Seoul quite well. That night Ted and I stayed at the Hospital. The next day Ted and I spent the day shopping around in the P.X. and Japanese Markets. That night the boys had another Bible study in a school building. So we went. It is interesting to see these young school children interested in the Bible. They had 10 or 12 each time. After Meeting Willis took Ted and I down town and we went in a real nice (fancy) Japanese Restaurant and had a Japanese dinner. That night we stayed at the Hospital. The next morning we got up early and met Don and Sproulie at the central station and went up to Nagoya. And spent a few hours with Cecil Barrett and Tom Stelfox. Tom is a Canadian boy. Had a very nice day together. We got back about ten o'clock that night and stayed at the Hospital again. Now on Sundays the boys always go out to Kyoto where there are two sister workers for meeting, Marquerite Sergeant and Shizuko Hoshina. So we went there for meeting. I have never enjoyed a meeting so much in my life I do not think so. There were us three soldiers and 4 workers. It sure was good to be with some workers again. Marquerite is a Canadian girl and Shizuko is a Japanese girl. (only 23 years old) and can not speak or understand English. Marquerite speaks Japanese though. So in the meeting she spoke Japanese. We had dinner with the girls. A very profitable day spent together. The workers seemed so pleased to have us and we were so happy to be there. There are no friends around that part of Japan. Only one boy which we met. He lives up where Cecil and Tommy are. So we certainly enjoyed the day. We went back to Camp. (as hard as it was). So all in all we had a very, very enjoyable time, I would not have missed the experience for anything. I could go on with ten more pages and still could not tell you but half of it but must close now. I must tell you I sent two boxes home from

Japan. Please let me know when you get them as I have them insured. It will take 6 to 8 weeks at least I suppose before you get them. I hope you like it! It was hard to come to Korea the first time. But almost worse to come back now. We were just dead tired and I slept most of the way on the plane and all afternoon here and still tired. Ha.

No more now, as this is a Japan Journal I guess. Hope all is well. Was glad for 3 of your letters today.

Love, Fritzie

Ted and I thoroughly enjoyed our time in Japan. Don Garland spoke some Japanese and agreed to take me shopping. I appreciated his help. We found a 12-piece serving set of Noritake Nippon Toki Kaisha dishes for my mother, and Don helped me ship them home; they all arrived in good condition. The dishes have always been an uplifting reminder of my trip to Japan. Joann and I now have the dishes since my mother passed away. On one occasion many years after the war, Don visited our home in Illinois and we served a meal on those dishes. The china provided for great conversation as we reminisced the war years.

The Sunday morning fellowship meeting in Kyoto, Japan was incredibly helpful. I felt strengthened, encouraged and filled with hope. Huge benefits were gained from a fairly small meeting: two minister women, two minister men, and three soldiers. As it turned out, it was the only fellowship meeting that I attended between July 1951 and April 5, 1953.

Cecil Barrett, Ted DeWitt, Tom Stelfox, Self, Don Garland
Sproulie Denio took the picture (family photo)

Ted and I returned to our military assignments in Korea knowing we made a good decision in our choice of rest and recuperation. The trip was a much needed realignment in the midst of a confusing experience. We had been refreshed. Letters from Sproulie and Don had deeper meaning after we met them. They asked many questions about conditions after the invasion. Clearly their hearts were still in Korea.

I was anxious to see some of the areas in Seoul that Sproulie and Don talked about. My assignment required me to make many trips to Seoul with my military transport vehicle. Sometimes I went to gather supplies, and sometimes a South Korean soldier needed to be transported from 121 Evac to the Korean hospital. These trips provided a bit of freedom and allowed me opportunity to learn my way around Seoul. City streets and directions became more familiar and I was able to locate places where the ministers had tried to help with the gospel. A local, young Korean boy helped me locate the address of Sproulie and Don's apartment. He found the location with relative ease and pointed out the house. Much to my surprise, it was barely damaged. Even though the city had changed control between the enemy and South Koreans four times in one year, somehow it escaped the bombs, rifle fire and heavy artillery. It seemed a miracle to me that the very house where the ministers had lived survived almost unscathed.

The two women pictured below were living in the apartment when I visited. They were acquainted with the ministers. I tried visiting with them, but due to the language barrier, I didn't understand much of what they were telling me. If I understood them correctly, the woman on the right owned the apartment.

Koreans near Sproulie and Don's apartment (family photo)

Back at the hospital Ted and I noticed another change after our return from Japan. A second lieutenant at the hospital was not nice or friendly; other soldiers did not like his attitude or demeanor. But after Ted and I returned from Japan, the officer was extremely friendly. He always spoke to me when we met on the grounds. I often wondered if he noticed something different in Ted and me from the other soldiers. I'll never know, and none of the other soldiers figured it out either. Rest and recuperation proved to have extended benefits. It remains a highlight of my entire military experience.

Heading to the Frontlines

Chapter 18
Taegu

Back at 121 Evac I began working again with Sam, the Korean man mentioned earlier, who took oranges home for his daughter. Sam told me about the place where he lived in Seoul before the war. When the war started he had to flee his home. He was not permitted to go back and see what damage was done, nor did he know if his home still existed. Sam and I had a good relationship, and I felt sorry for him and his family.

Sam knew that I sometimes took Korean patients to the Korean Hospital, and he asked me one day if I could take him along to Seoul so he could inspect his house. I wanted to do this for him, but it was against the rules to transport Korean civilians in military vehicles. I also knew that soldiers were punished for wrong doing. However, I helped Sam because, again, what were they going to do? Send me to Korea?

I knew I had to pass through an inspection point at the Han River, so I needed another plan. After I made sure my patients were comfortable in my vehicle, I wrapped Sam in extra blankets and made him look like another patient. I picked him up, placed him on a litter in the vehicle and I was ready to go. No problem with the MPs. They examined him just like the rest of my load and never knew what I had going on there. Once we were in Seoul, Sam got out and left to find his home. I continued on to a Seoul hospital and transferred the patients before returning to 121 Evac. Unfortunately I never saw Sam again. Perhaps this final opportunity to help Sam was a better farewell than words could have offered.

I was given one last assignment at 121 Evac. I was ordered to deliver a shipment of blood to a hospital in Taegu,

Korea. This was good news for me because it was an opportunity to visit my old friend, David Wahtly; a soldier I spent a lot of time with during basic training at Fort Meade.

With written orders in hand from my captain, I reported to the K12 Airport and requested a flight down to Taegu. A couple of pilots quickly responded to the captain's order and we were soon airborne with the shipment of blood. As I peered out the side window, I realized we had a US fighter jet escort just off the wingtip on the right side of the plane making for an interesting flight. I was fascinated with the close proximity of a fighter jet in flight because they were new to the military in this war. This jet was precise, powerful and produced the ultimate thrill of protection from the most powerful military in the world.

I delivered the blood to the hospital in Taegu, and thought I was free to find my way back to 121 Evac. So, without realizing any need for immediate return, I found my old friend, David. He was surprised to see me coming out of the middle of nowhere. We sat on the edge of the beds in his bunk, and talked that evening about old times at Fort Meade. We also enjoyed spiritual fellowship. It was an opportunity to express my gratitude for all the letters I received from his mother while in Korea. David said I could sleep on a bed next to his. When I asked about the soldier whose bed I occupied he responded, "Don't worry because that boy goes carousing in the village all night drinking Korean whisky." Next I worried a drunk soldier might return to the bunks and find me in his bed; then what? Again David calmly replied, "No problem. I will take care of him." So that was that, and I spent the night there. After sharing breakfast with David the next morning I began my journey back to 121 Evac.

Unfortunately, that was the last time I saw David. He returned to Louisiana after the war. Though his mother wrote me many letters, I never had the opportunity of meeting her. I wrote to David a few times, but he did not respond to my letters. Knowing I would be concerned when I didn't hear from him, David's sister wrote explaining that David no longer attended our fellowship meetings. These are the sad times in our lives.

The orders I received for Taegu must not have included instructions for my return because I took advantage of the freedom I thought I had to find my own way back to 121 Evac. After leaving David at the hospital in Taegu, I walked to the tracks and found a train going north instead of requesting the pilots to fly me back. I wanted to use the opportunity to explore Korea a bit and felt adventurous. I saw people in everyday life and observed how the war affected them.

The train went slowly because the tracks were in poor condition as result of extensive war damage. With no train tracks close to 121 Evac, the last segment of my journey required a search for jeep drivers to bring me back to the hospital. Korea did not have many roads or vehicles at this time. The only available roads were bumpy ones made and used by the Army.

Little did I know my assignment at 121 Evac was about to end. I did not foresee a change, so there was no time to prepare. There was no time to say goodbye to people with whom I worked closely. My turn to serve on the frontline approached and I would soon join the soldiers who suffered the deadliest attacks from enemy fire. Although we were in the middle of a brutal war, 121 Evac was stationed back from frontline danger and my current duties at this location were relatively easy to fulfill. My main responsibility was ensuring the comfort and safety of wounded soldiers as I transported them from hospital to airport. Yet, I was trained at Fort Meade, MD to be a combat medic. An ominous foreshadowing of inevitability crept over me and I felt I would soon be sent north of Seoul to the frontlines of battle.

I was a happy soldier when I arrived back at 121 Evac, because of my recent time with David and my adventure along the Korean countryside. But much to my surprise, I found an unsettling condition. My euphoria was crushed when I was greeted with the news that I was AWOL, absent without leave, and in deep trouble. I was stunned by the news, but that's Army life. This situation caused an immediate change. I was told to quickly grab a duffel bag along with all my clothes because my location of duty was changing. What I feared became real; I was headed to the frontlines of battle.

Chapter 19
Assigned to the Frontline

The reassignment happened so fast I felt rather numb. The massive misunderstanding ate at me. Before rushing off, I thought I should clear up my recent AWOL situation, so I went to the Orderly Room. There I made it clear to the captain and others of high rank I was only returning from my obligation of delivering blood to Taegu. After given only a brief time for explanation, I loaded my clothes in a duffel bag and jumped into the Army truck; other soldiers were already in the truck waiting for me. I looked down from my seat in the truck and saw my friend, Ted Dewitt, standing there looking forlorn. I did not even have time to shake his hand or say goodbye; that was the last time I saw Ted.

Though I didn't know it at the time, this change destined me to be on the frontline in close combat until I received orders to return to the United States for discharge. My transfer came sometime in late September or early October of 1952 and I remained on the frontlines until early February 1953. I totaled an estimated 122 days under enemy fire assisting wounded soldiers.

Keeping track of the days was not easy. I wanted a small calendar to keep in my billfold. However, all the surrounding towns and stores were severely damaged and going into town to shop for such things was impossible. Eventually someone gave me a little datebook and every evening I tried marking off another day. Yet, even keeping up with a calendar became confusing because I was distracted with all of the stress and casualties of the frontline. As a result, from the day I was transported to the frontline until I departed Korea, I simply lost track of time.

The frontline remained in roughly the same location near the 38th parallel since July 1951. However, we were never told our exact location of service and we were not told where we were going as we rode along in the back of the military truck headed towards the frontline. Our small group of soldiers bounced along silently lost in our thoughts of what may lie ahead. Night soon fell and the moon shone through the darkness. The position of the moon indicated we were heading north; the direction of the frontline from Seoul. At one point during the night, the driver stopped the truck and instructed us to get out and find a place to sleep for the remainder of the night. Though we questioned our exact location, we knew we were close to the frontline because we heard the big guns in the distance.

In the morning we loaded up and proceeded along the rutted road toward the frontline. After several hours we arrived at a small camp that was still a little ways back from frontline action. The big guns were much louder, but we could not see any fighting. Staccato eruptions of smaller weapons, punctuated with the percussion of the big guns, made us anxious. Combat stress had begun. We camped there for three or four days and waited aimlessly for further orders.

Captain Brown eventually arrived and delivered our orders. In his briefing he told us we were going to leave the camp after it got dark. He was not a friendly man and actually appeared quite mean. The only truly memorable thing he said projected his nasty demeanor. He had a 45 caliber pistol on the right side of his combat belt. He patted the gun with his right hand and said, "During our march up to the trenches and bunkers to relieve others who've been there for awhile, if any one of you men turn and start to run back I will shoot you with this weapon!" After his motivational speech we filtered back into camp, collected our things and waited for nightfall.

Darkness settled in and we were soon called to form a column and marched toward our frontline positions. As we arrived and relieved exhausted soldiers, we noticed that Captain Brown was nowhere to be seen. Each one had their own thoughts about what happened to the captain that evening. The soldiers with me hated him and his disrespectful behavior. We never saw Captain Brown again.

The march north went well that night in the dark. We marched past the large caliber guns along the way and there was some action that night. The big guns fired over us as we marched up to the trenches. My war experience had escalated again and I began adjusting to another new situation.

The medic I was ordered to replace got a break from the frontline action and now I was surrounded by the reality of active war. There was an unofficial saying that filtered through the troops: "If you make it through the first night, you'll likely make it at least a week. Make it through the first week and you'll likely make it at least a month. Make it through the first month and you'll likely make it home." I was keenly aware of my inexperience as I contemplated my responsibilities as the medic for all the infantrymen online at that location. Each medic was responsible for a section of the frontline. To be quickly available when needed, we tried to stay near the center of the section of our responsibility. Other medics were responsible where my line ended.

Trenches gave us some measure of safety. I took the following picture in 1990. The rise of dirt where I have my right hand provided stability for the barrel of the weapons.

Soldiers had some protection behind the dirt, yet they could see over the mound to fire on any enemy advance. Below are two photos showing the "then and now." The trees in the recent picture have all grown up since the war ended.

Frontline trenches (historical military photo and 1990 family photo)

Soldiers before us also built bunkers for safety. My sergeant was a machine gunner, and was very skilled at anchoring his weapon and keeping the enemy at a distance. He also used the buildup of dirt to position the barrel of the machine gun.

There was another man we met upon arriving at the frontline. I don't remember the lieutenant's name, but he was much different from Captain Brown. He was admirable for several reasons. Every time we met up, whether in the field or in the trenches, he always had a pleasant and respectful greeting when I saluted him. I do not know if he showed respect to me because I was a frontline medic with great responsibility, or if he treated every soldier this way.

But I do know that not all lieutenants were like him. He was as tall as me and walked like he was in a soldier's parade even when he was in the trenches. I never saw him when the action was at the greatest, but he always carried his rifle slung vertical with his body while keeping one hand on the trigger. I always enjoyed speaking with him. It would be a real joy to meet up with him again someday. Many times I wished that I had a camera with me on the frontline. This man was a good image of a soldier.

As a combat medic, it was inevitable I would soon receive my first casualty. We were engaged in serious action against the enemy with a lot of lead flying both directions. Soldiers called it a "dog fight." The communists tried many times to push us south and gain more land and property for themselves. I noticed one soldier acting strangely as he tried to walk with one foot injured. I went closer to him and saw a hole in his left foot. I quickly realized this soldier could not handle frontline war action and had lost it mentally. He was one of our own American soldiers, but the poor soul had shot a hole in his own foot. I quickly grabbed his rifle so he could not shoot himself again, or me for that matter, before I examined his foot.

I told him to put his left hand on my right shoulder to lighten the weight on his injured foot. I could not see anything more to do with the injury at that time; it was more important to get him out of there. I told him to hang onto me and we went over the mountain crest and down the back side to the aid station. He maybe thought that an injury would get him free from all of this. And it did.

Evacuating the soldier required climbing out of the trenches and making a dash for the crest. We were exposed during this time with the possibility of being hit with enemy fire. Recollection of the situation fades at this point. My memory of many frontline experiences ends this way. I remember up to a certain point, but the rest is gone. Perhaps it is a blessing. The scenes were usually more terrifying and traumatizing than gory. Recalling it in detail would cause me to relive it. My mind may have fallen apart a long time ago and I wouldn't be much different than this soldier. Anyway, that was my first wounded soldier.

Chapter 20
Combat Medics

Combat medics served in many capacities including aid stations and field hospitals, but battlefield medical support was the primary focus. Fort Mead training for medics included important adherence to international rules when at war with another nation. These rules were established in Geneva, Switzerland in 1864 by the Geneva Convention, International Committee of the Red Cross. The purpose of these rules is to protect any victims of the war such as prisoners of war, wounded soldiers, refugees, civilians and other non-combatants who have reason to be near a war zone.

When treating an injured soldier on the battlefield, the enemy, according to the rules, was not to use weapons of any kind to further cause injury to the wounded or the medic administering first aid. This protection was also supposed to cover all equipment and vehicles being used to evacuate injured soldiers. Medical evacuation vehicles were to be marked with a large red cross. Combat medics were also issued red and white armbands for this reason, hoping to be respected by the enemy as wounded soldiers were removed from combat.

However, we were told that the enemy we faced in Korea did not know or respect the Geneva Convention rules. The following picture is a United States Army ambulance heavily riddled by communist small arms and automatic weapons in Korea. Such evidence proves a graphic example of the complete disregard by the communists of the international rules of warfare providing safe passage of all vehicles identified with a red cross and used to transport the wounded.

This United States Army ambulance, heavily riddled by Communist small arms and automatic weapons fire in Korea, is a graphic example of the complete disregard of the Communists of those international rules of warfare providing for the safe passage of all vehicles identified with a Red Cross and used to transporting the wounded.

K D Army ambulance (Song, p.16)

I was issued a red and white armband but I never used it in combat. It would have only made a good target for the ill-informed enemy not honoring the rules. I still have the armband today.

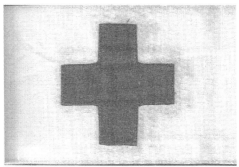

Armband issued for the combat medic (family photo)

As a combat medic, there are certain reflections I doubt I will ever forget. Some of these things are my own thoughts and feelings, and some result from sharing war experiences with other combat medics. Below is a summary of a few reflections:

- It is not miraculous technology that saves lives on the battlefield! The most important tool is the tourniquet.
- Short-term use of tourniquets can save soldiers who would otherwise die of blood loss.
- Medics must use any resource available to them.
- Medics learn quickly to solve problems - plug the leaks, stop the bleeding - speed is the key.
- War medicine is not civilian medicine because the wounds are worse.
- There are no restrictions on the battlefield - do the best that you can and hope it works.
- Life is everything - it is all that matters - details come later.
- Combat medics and nurses are doing things in the field that only doctors do in the States.
- Medicine is more advanced than ever, but it cannot wipe out the brutality of the battlefield.

Combat medics were issued bullet-proof vests to be worn when going into combat with other troops. I observed many lives that were saved by these vests. They were made to protect a soldier's chest and back. Small-arms fire could not penetrate the vest. It was no problem wearing it night and day. I appreciated the satisfaction of protection. A person never knew when the enemy would attack. You had to always be prepared and alert. The enemy always tried to surprise and attack when we were the least prepared.

Many techniques were used to protect our lives. In one example, the British used a dog troop, run by the Royal Engineers. Some of the animals were trained to detect mines. Others were trained to look for wounded men. Most successful of all were the patrol dogs trained to detect the presence of the enemy. Some of the dogs were capable of detecting an enemy up to 400 yards away. In the midst of a patrol battle and with the sound of gunfire, the dogs were able to detect Chinese ambush positions more than 30 yards away. Regardless of all the effort, war is dangerous and brutal and the combat medic provided the hope of preserving the wounded soldier's life.

Medics carrying a wounded soldiers
Left - (CDRS)   Right - (Learning Centre)

Pictured are combat medics carrying wounded soldiers on their backs. It shows how I carried the wounded in Korea. We could not use a jeep in Korea because of mountainous terrain. After I reduced their pain and stopped the bleeding, I picked them up, carried them over the mountain crest and brought them to the aid station.

The evacuation system used in Korea was first developed during the American Civil War by Dr. Jonathan Letterman (1824 – 1872). Dr. Letterman was an American surgeon who is credited with originating the modern methods for medical organization in armies. He is considered the "Father of Battlefield Medicine," and his system made it possible for thousands of wounded men to be recovered and treated. Many of the technologies and techniques used today were not available in Korea. Still, we saved many lives.

Military medics are a fairly recent development in history. Survival rates of wounded soldiers has increase dramatically as this part of the military has improved. The article below provides historical context.

A Brief History of Military Medics

During Ancient times if a soldier was wounded, he laid in the field where he had fallen. There was no one to come to his aid.

Napoleon's Army was the first to assign people to help the wounded. They were called the litter-bearers, made up mostly of inept and expendable soldiers. The American Colonial Army lead by George Washington, also had litter-bearers during the Revolutionary War.

In 1862, due to the unexpected size of casualty lists during the battle of Manassas where it took one week to remove the wounded from the battlefield, Dr. Jonathan Letterman, Head of Medical Services of the Army of the Potomac, revamped the Army Medical Corps. His contribution included staffing and training men to operate horse teams and wagons to pick up wounded soldiers from the field and to bring them back to field dressing stations for initial treatment. This was our Nation's first Ambulance Corps. Dr. Letterman also developed the 3 tiered evacuation system which is still used today. Field Dressing (Aid) Station - located next to the battlefield. Dressings and tourniquets Field Hospital - Close to the battlefield (during the Civil War it would be Barns or Houses, today they are known as MASH units). Emergency surgery and treatment, Large Hospital - Away from the battlefield.

For patients' prolonged treatment, Dr. Letterman's transportation system proved successful. In the battle of Antietam, which was a 12 hour engagement and the bloodiest one day battle in the entire Civil War, the ambulance system was able to remove all the wounded from the field in 24 hours. Dr. Jonathan Letterman is known today as the Father of Modern Battlefield Medicine. Unfortunately, amputation was the primary method of treatment for wounds to extremities during the Civil War with over 50,000 resulting amputees. During the Spanish American War in the 1890's Nicholas Sin stated, "Fate of the wounded soldier is determined by the hand which applies the dressing. Field dressings are now applied by litter-bearers in the field." World War I required millions of casualties to be treated at the front. Unlike previous wars, battles did not stop to retrieve the wounded or the dead.

World War I saw for the first time medics rushing forward with the troops, finding the wounded, stopping their bleeding and bringing the wounded soldier to the aid station. In World War I medics were no longer expendable and were well trained. After World War I, military medicine advanced. Training became a priority both in fighting and medical care. Medics were trained with infantry soldiers, learning how to use the lay of the land for their protection and that of their patients. Medics were also trained in the use of pressure dressings, plasma IV's, tracheotomies, splints, and administering drugs.

During World War II a wounded soldier had an 85% chance of surviving if he was treated by a medic within the first hour. This figure was three times higher than World War I survival statistics. The red cross worn by medics on their helmet and arm bands became visible targets for enemy snipers during World War II and Korea. Korea saw the advent of the helicopter being used to bring men from the frontlines to M*A*S*H units (Mobile Army Surgical Hospital). In Vietnam, the medic's job was to treat and evacuate. Medevac helicopters now could bring medics on board to continue treating the wounded while transporting them back to the Field Hospitals. There was a 98% survival rate for soldiers who were evacuated within the first hour. Vietnam was the first time medics were armed and carried firearms and grenades into combat. Red crosses on helmets and arm bands were no longer worn. (Vigilant Hunter Brigade, para. 1)

The Korean War had the new advantage of evacuation helicopters. Combat medics provided battlefield first aid and carried the injured to nearby aid stations. Evacuation helicopters transported the wounded soldiers from aid stations to hospitals located away from the main hostilities. Rarely were they used to pick up a wounded soldier directly in the battlefield.

Medical team for forward position (Olive-Drab)

Medical evacuation helicopter (Olive-Drab)

The speed of evacuation by helicopters was a major factor in saving many lives.

Chapter 21
Frontline Action

Many people have questioned me about fear experienced under combat conditions. I believe any man who has seen combat and claims he never felt fear is either crazy or lying. As for me, I've had difficulty remembering some of the frontline events. Maybe it is good that some of the pain and blood I saw and dealt with are gone. Perhaps more importantly, I no longer have to relive the terrifying and traumatizing situations where I could have been a casualty. I appreciated a quote by Ambrose Redmoon, "Courage is not the absence of fear! Rather, courage comes from a reserve of mind more powerful than outside circumstances. Courage is the judgment that something else is more important than fear. Freedom is the sure possession of those alone who have the courage to defend it!" (PJ Lighthouse, Sect 10)

The days and nights were sometimes calm with little or no enemy action. Warfare wasn't continuous. Quiet periods presented challenges of staying vigilant. It was evident to me we were there to keep the communists to the north and not let them come south again like they did two times prior.

There were day and night patrols. The day patrols looked for hidden enemy soldiers who came over during the night and posed a threat to soldiers and Korean civilians. The night patrols looked for enemy soldiers in "no man's" territory trying to get over to our side. Periodically I participated in both of these patrols.

One evening my sergeant and I were commanded to conduct a search in "no man's" territory and report to the commanding officer. I do not remember why, and I don't think we were told what had happened that prompted the search. My sergeant was a machine gunner and also had a small caliber rifle instead of an M-1 rifle. I was surprised to be chosen for this particular patrol because I carried no weapons. Maybe a medic was chosen in the event we came upon a wounded soldier who was missing in action. My sergeant did not seem too concerned when he realized I wasn't carrying a gun. I guess he thought he could handle any situation with his rifle.

In the darkness of the night, I remember walking very slowly with my sergeant. We whispered to each other attempting to keep directions straight while at the same time fearing we might walk into a camp of communists. It went well until we heard voices in the distance; voices coming from enemy territory. We could not run because of limited vision, nor did we have much time to plan a quiet escape. But I remember seeing a nearby stack of brush under which we very quickly crawled and quietly remained until the enemy passed. We heard them talking, but because of the language barrier we could not understand what they said. We caught glimpses of their eyes as they passed; they came much too close for our comfort. Our long and arduous wait continued until the enemy was out of earshot and we crawled out from under the brush pile. Not knowing which direction they took added to our continued anxiety of surviving night patrol that evening.

However, no more excitement ensued and we returned to our own frontline before daylight. I never heard more about our night patrol and why my sergeant and I had to do it. However, night patrols were important and serious business. A quote from another soldier illustrates this point: "Barely a night passed without a fiercely contested patrol encounter in no man's land" (Hickey, p. 253).

I received two kinds of training: infantry training and combat medic training. Now I experienced both in action. Infantry training is all about protecting our country and defending oneself as well as those around us. Combat medics were trained to provide immediate assistance for wounded soldiers. Stop the bleeding, treat for shock, give pain relief and remove injured soldiers from the frontline. A combat medic stays right with the infantry and shares the same war experiences. In addition, the medic also has intense experiences with the wounded. It is difficult to describe the feelings of working one-on-one with the injured and dying soldiers; doing everything you know to try and preserve life and hope. I believe the extra training of two boot camps helped save my life in more than one occasion.

Another time I found myself in a foxhole with a soldier during intense fighting. We were in the midst of using all the means available to stop the communists from advancing further south. A lot of lead flew in both directions. Ahead of us was a soldier who was shot down and not able to get up. He screamed with pain and fear. As I left the foxhole to help him, I glanced back briefly only to see the remaining soldier struck with a hand grenade. Within mere seconds, I was responsible for two injured soldiers and narrowly escaped my own casualty. I crawled back in the foxhole and gave a shot of morphine, but it was immediately evident his injuries were very severe and he would not live. Given the triage situation, I decided to go help the other soldier.

Once I got to the other soldier, I realized he had sustained a painful back injury keeping him from walking. He was out of the trench so we were exposed to enemy fire and our troops fired heavily to hold down the enemy. Being unable to use jeeps to carry wounded soldiers, I lifted him onto my back and started the climb toward the crest of the mountain on the way to the aid station.

We didn't get far before I saw my exit route, my only obvious escape, exploding with mortar shells. Behind me I heard mortars leave enemy guns sounding like a cork being pulled out of a bottle. When we heard that noise, we "hit the dirt" and waited as the mortars passed overhead. They exploded the path where I planned carrying the injured soldier. I could not see a way to get this soldier to safety. I remembered being told in training to stay low. Looking at the "V" shape of the mortar explosion I saw it was safer close to the ground. Bent low with the soldier on my back, I ran for it while choosing a direction and hoping to weave between the mortar blasts. That is where my memory stops. I cannot tell you any more about either one of my patients. I have been told by my loved ones that is nature's way of dealing with overwhelming traumatic situations. However, in this case I am convinced that my training saved my life.

Another time, my sergeant and I stood in the trench together when it was quiet and without combat action; a lull in the day. We both looked north toward enemy land and to our great surprise, one of our own fighter planes flew right over us. Just a short distance past us, the pilot released a bomb. We saw it fall and watched everything on the ground, including buildings, explode upward. The air filled with dust, dirt and shattered pieces of shelters, but there were also arms and legs. The enemy was human too. We felt a flood of confused emotions; the plane was exciting, the accuracy of the awesome explosion was exhilarating, yet the moment shocking, dreadful and at the same time, very sobering. It was the first time I saw a bomb dropped and exploded. The pilot turned to the right and was quickly gone out of sight.

All happened so fast it was hard to comprehend the destruction. We didn't hear enemy guns respond. Our pilot must have made a direct hit. This was the first war in which performance jet aircraft were used in combat. Many lessons were learned.

At times, the unthinkable added stress and challenge for soldiers engaged in close combat on the ground. Local civilians were often employed by the Army to carry meals from the supply stations to the frontline. The enemy, if allowed the chance, killed the Korean civilian hired to deliver meals to the front. Then, wearing the civilian's clothing, the enemy snuck up on us, pulled out his weapon, and shot our soldiers before we had time to respond. I never saw this happen, but other soldiers reported it so the rest of us could be warned. Again, our survival depended upon working together to protect and defend each other.

I remember one time another soldier and I pulled branches over a large hole to create camouflage and protection from the enemy. Bullets started hitting the ground only a few feet from our desired place of safety. Knowing the enemy aimed for us, we quickly ran to a safer place. I never returned to that spot again.

The Chinese experimented with tunnels for shock attacks. Thousands of Chinese soldiers toiled and dug remarkable tunnels with plans to surface for battle at surprise locations. They planned on tunneling through mountains where they could establish headquarters, field hospitals and supply dumps. Theoretically, there were miles and miles of tunnels where whole battalions rested secure from even the heaviest bombing or artillery fire. In the end, the tunnels did not become a major factor, but they made us aware we had to use all means possible to be watchful and protect human life.

Once, the medic on my right got word to me that he needed help. I worked my way over and crawled down in the bunker where he assisted a wounded soldier. Dealing with the sight was very difficult. The wounded soldier was shot in the groin and was bleeding badly. We had to find a way to stop the bleeding. Again, my mind is blank on how we handled the situation. All I remember is the blood I saw and the helpless feeling not knowing where to apply pressure to stop the bleeding. The soldier's life was just leaking out from what could have been a survivable injury.

Fortunately our time on the frontline was not always traumatic. However, it was always stressful. We were never sure what might happen next and we always felt a bit on edge. When it was calm during a lull between combat activity, medics acted as doctors for minor scratches, colds, headaches and the like. Help was given as best we could with aspirin and bandages.

Periodically our military captured enemy soldiers. We removed weapons and searched clothing for possible hand grenades. Then we made sure our prisoners were securely guarded to prevent escape or harm to ourselves. We did not torture prisoners in any way; even if they did not cooperate with us. On one occasion I remember an enemy soldier who was not in agreement with anything we tried to do. Using a tree limb as a pole, we tied his feet and hands together around the limb so we could carry him down the mountain instead of walking with him.

Eventually the captives were sent to an island off the South Korean coast. Sometimes they tried to swim back to the mainland, but soldiers on guard boats did not allow it.

After the war when I managed the building business in Illinois, I met a Korean veteran who was assigned to a guard boat. He told me he shot his rifle many times to hit the water ahead of the swimming prisoners, but never intended to kill them. The prisoners would turn around and swim back to the island as fast as they could.

Frontline duty did not allow for personal time. Every soldier's duty was important as we stayed vigilant. We learned to shave under improvised conditions. When there were lulls, no enemy action, we melted snow in our helmets which became our makeshift pots. With the melted snow water, we washed our faces and shaved.

I only remember taking a shower one time that winter. On the edge of a village, a temporary shower was built outside in the open. We lined up in one row and were asked to remove all clothing. One by one each soldier was permitted to walk to the shower. The local village people observed the whole operation. Once we were through the shower, we were given nice clean and dry clothing. They felt so good after living and sleeping indefinitely in the ones we just removed. We returned to the frontlines and relieved others so they too could enjoy the shower and the clean clothes. This happened when the action on the frontline was close to zero, and then only a few of us went at a time.

Time wore on as we went about our frontline duties. We took it one day at a time and simply did the best we could as each situation presented itself.

Chapter 22
War Conditions and the Frontline

Winter conditions on the frontline were especially difficult. By the time I arrived, it was nearly impossible to keep warm during the Manchurian winter. It didn't really matter how many layers of clothing we wore. Poor footwear sentenced hundreds of men to death as my American comrades dealt with temperatures of minus 35 degrees. Many victims succumbed to frostbite and trench foot, a condition caused by prolonged exposure to cold, wet and unsanitary conditions. In sub-zero temperatures the engines of all vehicles froze solid unless started every half hour through the night. Of course, our weapons also required additional attention in the extreme cold conditions. We fired automatic weapons every 15 minutes to prevent trouble.

Left - Snow on the frontline (About.com, image 45)
Middle & Right - Wait and watching in the snow (Olive-Drab)

I was told the soldiers who fought early in the war did not have adequate clothing for the North Korean climate which caused a lot of pain and suffering. I heard much about frostbite and toes that required amputation, but did not witness such conditions among the soldiers around me. We were issued white coveralls after it snowed with instructions to wear them over the top of our clothing; orders from headquarters so that the enemy could not spot us in the snow.

Growing up in Illinois with lots of snow made it easier to survive the harsh conditions in Korea. We built bunkers, or protective dugouts, close to the trenches on the frontline. Bunkers gave us some protection from the enemy as well as from the harsh winter weather. A bunker was usually large enough for two or more soldiers to retreat when it was quiet. Tree limbs and branches were placed over the dugouts to keep some of the wind and snow away from us. At night when there was little or no action from the enemy, one of us had a place to get a little sleep while the other one stayed outside to watch for those who tried to do away with us.

We frequently had unwelcomed guests in our bunkers. Rats seemed to think the bunkers were built for them, too. While very plentiful in that part of the country, rats somehow knew there might be a little food in the bunker. So it was not unusual for a rat to fall out of the makeshift roof of branches and land right on my face while I tried to sleep. We were trained for combat, and I was trained as a combat medic, but the Army failed to train us to fend off rats when they landed on our faces in the middle of the night.

In our efforts to keep warm, we often built a little fire inside our bunker during cold winter nights. I remember one specific occasion when another soldier and I were both inside the bunker with what we thought to be a "little" fire kindled. Another soldier came down into our bunker and warned that sparks from our fire shot upward several feet high making a good target for the enemy. Thanking the one who informed us, we put out that fire without delay.

During the winter we lost some of our soldiers to a strange type of illness that no one seemed to understand at the time. Among the troops it was called "hemorrhagic fever" because of the symptomatic and persistently high fever. Though there was no proof at the time, soldiers thought it came from the rats. Sadly, we had no way to treat the illness that often caused death. After I came home from Korea, I asked my doctor about the hemorrhagic fever problem. He never heard of it. However, today it is recognized as the Korean hemorrhagic fever, and is known to be a very serious virus carried by rodents; a silent killer. I guess the soldiers had it right after all.

A bombing (About.com, image 46 and 51)

Many times I saw a similar sight to the above picture while I stood in a trench and watched a fighter pilot fly over us very low. The bomb dropped in enemy territory. We were close enough to see and hear it hit the target.

(Army History, para. 13 and 27)

The mountainous landscape in the background of the above pictures is a true representation of the terrain I experienced when I transported wounded soldiers from the frontline back to the aid station. Though I don't have my own photos of this part of the war, these guns were constantly fired as I carried the wounded to an aid station.

Supplies and soldiers protecting the supplies (family photos)

Supplies and soldiers protecting the supplies (family photos)

We also had to provide protection for our frontline supplies. Trucks brought necessary materials and supplies to designated locations back a ways from the frontline. The supplies consisted of: ammunition, clothing, footwear, medical, guns, food, personal, and perhaps other things I'm not remembering. The support in the background of our war effort was very necessary in sustaining our efforts on the frontline. Those of us who were on the front could not leave our place of responsibility for fear of the enemy coming, destroying life and taking land that was not theirs. We were very grateful to those who guarded our supplies and supported our efforts.

Our food was also prepared at these supply locations which presented another reason why these areas were under guard. Meals were never brought to us at the same time. When the enemy was given a chance to recognize a pattern, they attacked during a time when we might be more relaxed. The enemy would try anything and a person always had to be on guard. Life on the frontline consisted of countless hours of anxious waiting punctuated by periods of intense and confusing action.

The enemy also tried to discourage us with propaganda leaflets. I saw many of these leaflets which were intended to dishearten soldiers while the Chinese Army attempted to persuade American soldiers to surrender to the North Koreans.

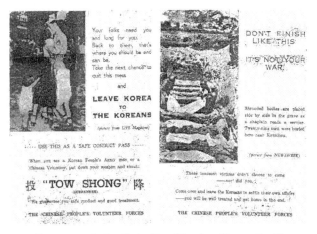

Propaganda leaflets (PsyWarrior, Example 7)

Conditions on the frontline were rough. I arrived on the frontlines in October 1952, remained until early February 1953, and never saw a bed during that time. It was very cold. Much of my time on the frontline is a blur today. Yet, we were cared for and every possible precaution was taken to protect us. I remember we were given at least one good meal every day and the food was reasonably enjoyable.

As I reflect upon the experience now, I believe there was a reason for the timing of my transfer to the frontline. A short time before my reassignment, a colonel was sent to Korea who did not agree with the Army about the CO classification. He did not believe a CO should be considered a soldier in the line-of-duty; rather, he believed there was no place for such a classification in the military. I was told that he passed an order that all COs in Korea would be sent to the frontlines for duty. So in addition to my AWOL experience, I feel that colonel was another reason for my change of duties.

I am neither angry nor disappointed that my war experience included months of time on the frontline. It put me in a position to help wounded solders who could not help themselves. With honor, I can truly say that I am thankful for the experience and the knowledge that it gave me.

Chapter 23
"Killed in Action"

The first day of every month was payday for soldiers, even on the frontline. Not too far back from the trenches a payroll captain occupied an Army tent. We went in one at a time to receive our wages, cash in US dollars. I believe we were paid about $38 per month, and soldiers under enemy fire on the frontline received additional pay. At the time I thought it odd that frontline soldiers were paid in cash even though we had nowhere to spend it, and we of course didn't know how long we would be out there accumulating monthly wages in cash. Since the US Army also made arrangements to have money forwarded back to the US, I gave the payroll captain instructions to send my earnings home to my mother. The Army required us to confirm these directions every month when we went to collect our pay.

I clearly recall the day I collected my wages in December, 1952. It started out like any other payday in the Army. As we were trained, I walked into the tent and saluted the captain saying, "Donald R. Borgman reporting for pay, sir." The captain responded, "At ease, soldier." Then what seemed ordinary soon became puzzling. The captain informed me, "I am sorry soldier, but I do not have any money for you today." Next he proceeded to tell me I was "killed in action." Clearly, a mistake was made, names were confused and I reportedly died. That ended my monthly stipend for a while.

US Army records indicated I lost my life on November 5, 1952. Unfortunately, my parents received this distressing news on November 10 by a telegram sent from the US Army.

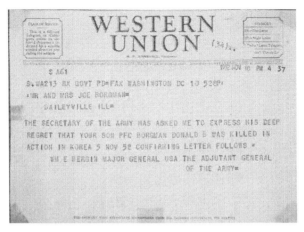

Telegram sent to my parents

Though the details of my death were scant, many newspaper articles were published about the Baileyville soldier who died while serving in Korea. Below is a sampling of the clippings my mother saved.

Baileyville Soldier Killed In Korea

BAILEYVILLE — Pfc. Donald Borgman, 23, son of Mr. and Mrs. Joe Borgman of Baileyville, was killed in action in Korea on Nov. 5, according to word received Monday night by his parents.

Pfc. Borgman, who entered the Army 19 months ago, was on duty with the Medical Corps. He had been overseas for 18 months and was due to be discharged in February.

He was born July 30, 1929, in Freeport, the only child of Mr. and Mrs. Joe Borgman. He attended grade school at German Valley and was graduated from Forreston High School in 1947. Between his graduation from high school and his entry into the service, he was employed at the Classey Feed Mill in Baileyville.

No details of his death were given in the telegram.

The only immediate survivors are his parents.

BAILEYVILLE GI DIES IN ACTION

Parents Notified

(Consolidated News Service)

BAILEYVILLE — Pfc. Donald Borgman, 23, Baileyville, a medical corpsman, was killed in action in Korea Nov. 5, according to a defense department telegram received Tuesday by his parents, Mr. and Mrs. Joseph Borgman.

The Baileyville soldier entered the army 19 months ago and had been overseas 18 months. He was slated to be discharged in February.

Borgman, an only child, was born in Freeport. He attended grade school in Germany Valley and graduated from Forreston high school in 1947. Before entering the army, he was employed at the Classey feed mill, Baileyville.

Baileyville Soldier Killed in Korea. PFC Donald Borgman, Baileyville, was killed in action in Korea on Nov. 5, according to word received Monday night by his parents. PFC Borgman, who entered the Army 19 months ago, was on duty with the Medical Corps. He had been overseas for 18 months and was due to be discharged in Feb. No details of his death were given in the telegram.

Of course my mother and dad were devastated. Many of my relatives, in a state of denial, questioned if I really was dead. They couldn't accept the tragic news about Joe and Gertie's only son. Some of them even consulted a "witch doctor" inquiring about my wellbeing. The doctor, whom I never met, described what I looked like and assured my relatives I was still alive. However, knowing my parents did not believe in such black magic, this event was never told to them and I learned of it only after my mother's death. So without this knowledge and after discussing it with my father, one of my uncles decided it was his elected duty to look inside the casket when it arrived to confirm that it really was my body before making any funeral arrangements.

My parents lived in misery and grief for four days before the US Army corrected the mistake by sending two officers with notification of the error. Learning of the error was a huge relief, but my parents were now very concerned about my safety. Below is a sampling of the newspaper articles explaining the US Army's correction. In addition to these articles there were many others printed with inaccurate information about the incident.

Killed in Action

GI Reported Killed in Action Still Alive, Parents Are Told

(Consolidated News Service)

FORRESTON — The parents of a Baileyville medical corpsman, who had been reported killed in Korean combat Nov. 5, learned Friday that their son is still alive.

A defense department telegram notified the parents, Mr. and Mrs. Joseph Borgman, Baileyville, that their only son, Donald, 23, was not killed in action. The wire stated he was still serving with frontline troops.

"This is wonderful — it's just more than words can tell," Mrs. Borgman exclaimed after learning that her son had virtually "returned from the dead." Her voice quivered with excitement.

Word of their son's safety came to the Borgmans a year and a day after he landed in Korea to serve with the 179th regiment, 45th infantry division. Pfc. Borgman was in Japan about six months before going to Korea.

Last Tuesday, the Borgmans received a defense department telegram reporting their son's death in Korea, but Friday's telegram declared this report erroneous. There was no explanation of how the mixup occurred.

Pfc. Borgman entered the army 19 months ago and has been overseas 18 months. He was slated to be discharged in April.

He was born in Freeport and attend Germany Valley schools before graduating from Freeport high school in 1947. Before entering the army, he was employed in the Classey feed mill, Baileyville.

Donald Borgman Not Killed in Korean Fighting

The best news ever received by a family in this community was doubtless that second message received by Mr. and Mrs. Joe Borgman of Baileyville last Friday afternoon, telling them their only son, Donald, was not a war casualty but was all right and on regular duty. The first message came Armistice Tuesday telling that Donald had been lost in the active fighting on the Korean battle front.

It now appears he had lost his identification number. This was presumably found by another soldier, was turned in at headquarters, and by some error it was then reported that Donald had been lost in action.

Not only do they have the reassuring message but they have also received two letters written by him since Armistice Day.

Donald is a member of the 1947 class of FCHS, 11 of whose members have been in or are now in the armed forces: Eldon Shellhause, who was wounded in Korea last April; Collin Chriss, now in Germany; Henry Genandt in North Africa; Gordon Gravenstein in Alaska; Robert Bear, Robert Dietz, Glenn Greenfield, and James Kancy, who are all in the states yet. Jay Rebel and Donald Wernick have completed their period of service.

Baileyville Soldier 'Returns From Dead' On Government Error

BAILEYVILLE—Three days of sorrow turned into more joy "than words can tell" Friday for Mr. and Mrs. Joseph Borgman of Baileyville, when they were informed that an earlier telegram listing their son, Donald, 23, as a Korean victim, was erroneous.

Friday's message informed the Baileyville couple that their only son had not been killed in action, but was still serving in the frontlines. Last Tuesday they had been informed that their son, a medical corpsman, had been killed in action on Nov. 5.

The sudden reversal left the Borgman home seething with excitement. "This is wonderful—it's just more than words can tell," said Mrs. Borgman.

There was no explanation of how the error had occurred.

Pfc. Borgman, who has been overseas for 18 months, is scheduled to be discharged in the spring. He is serving with the 179th regiment, 45th infantry division.

Interestingly though, my parents received a letter from me during the four days I was presumed dead. My letter was dated after I was supposedly killed. Along with the Army's acknowledgement of their error, my letter helped assure mother and dad I really was still alive. Albeit, not necessarily safe.

Because I was the last one in my family to receive news of my death, I was completely unaware all this was going on in Baileyville. Prior to requesting my wages that December day, I had no reason to suspect my family experienced four difficult days of grief. Below is the letter my mother wrote trying to explain the situation from my family's point of view.

Nov. 22, 1952.

Our Dearest Donald:

This will be an unusual letter, but it has come to where we must tell you what happened Nov. 10. The war department gave us some terrible news when they sent us a telegram telling us you had been killed in action. We cannot tell it in words when 4 days later 2 officers (soldiers) from Rockford came and told us it was an error. How happy we were then – but we did suffer from shock and surely we could not ever go through such again and we feel the need of getting you out of a combat area. We went to the Red Cross and you will find the enclosed paper. [I do not have that paper] The Red Cross told us that you would need to go to your commanding officers and ask for a reassignment to a non–combat area. The enclosed papers are all ready. Give them all to your commanding officers. Tell them that you are our only child and that dad has a heart condition and etc. I do not know now if I have made this plain to you, but do not worry over us. We tried for an emergency leave – but we cannot get it so this is the best we can do to get you out of that area.

We did not like to tell you about this because we do not want you to worry over us, but it is the fear we have that moves us to do this. Your letters have been a wonderful comfort to us and that is why we ask you to write often. We wrote you a letter this morning and will try and write another one tomorrow – only wanted to get this started and wrote in a hurry.

Our deepest love!

Ma and Dad

The Red Cross has also sent a letter to the Adjutant General at Washington.

Mother's letter

Naturally, my parents were very concerned about me after this experience, and wanted me reassigned to a less dangerous, non–combat area. Below is a copy of the letter my father wrote asking for a reassignment, but I do not know to whom it was sent.

> *Borgman, Donald Ray PFC:*
> *To whom it may concern:*
>
> *Due to recent events we are requesting consideration of reassignment of our son, the above captioned, to a non-combat area.*
> *On Nov. 10th 1952 we were advised by Adjutant General Office that our son had been killed in service. On Nov. 14th we were visited by a representative of that office that the message was in error and our son had returned to duty.*
> *You can readily understand our great concern since Donald is our only child. He had been in service since April, 1951 and in Korea since Nov. 1951. We are not asking for his release from military service until he has fulfilled his enlistment however we are greatly upset at this time and do urgently request that he be given a reassignment to an area where we would have a more secure feeling of reassurance for his safety.*
> *Joe Borgman*
> *Baileyville, Ill.*

I have copies of numerous letters written on my behalf for my parents in their attempt to have me reassigned to a safer location. One letter in particular was written by their doctor, N. C. Phillips, MD, who made it very clear my father should not be subjected to further emotional strain; he already suffered a coronary heart attack which disabled him for four months.

The efforts to get me reassigned were unrealistic, but I understood and deeply appreciated my parents' concern. They hoped that with the letters of support they collected and sent to me, I could request reassignment, and part of their nightmare would be over.

My poor mother and father had no idea what war was like on the frontline, especially in Korea. Any officer with the authority to reassign my position was a long ways from where I was trying to give a shot of morphine to wounded soldiers in a snow bank with lead flying in all directions. As a soldier, I was simply trying to survive flying bullets, grenades and bombs, while at the same time attempting to preserve life for the gravely wounded.

My parents, and everyone who wrote letters to the commanding officers, had no way of knowing that without an order, no reason permitted a combat medic in the trenches to walk away from his duties. There was no way I could take the handful of letters and papers to a commanding officer. Frankly, I don't recall even trying to find a commanding officer. I remember fearing if I tried, the US Army perhaps would lock me up in jail and punish me for walking away from injured soldiers and leaving my place of responsibility.

There is a part of every soldier's experience that cannot be easily told. My parents could not possibly have understood the grim aspects of my job as a medic on the frontline. Much of the death and suffering that took place, and the fear we lived with day in and day out, are a blur to me today. There is no way to fully explain the brutality of war. Only through experience can a person truly understand my story. I have struggled all my life with the challenge of explaining it. We questioned many times why we were there and what we were fighting for, but at the same time we attempted to maintain a perspective and remember that we were trying to win a war for the Korean people who could one day enjoy peace and liberty.

Going Home

Chapter 24
Aid Station Assignment

My Korean military involvement continually escalated. It began with hearing news about a Korean War at a time in my young life when I did not even know where this small Asian country was located. Soon thereafter I was drafted and began basic training. Each step marked a deeper commitment and brought experiences with long-lasting feelings for a young boy from Northern Illinois.

Participation in the war effort deepened with active duty in Korea and climaxed with several months of service on the frontline where I served as a medic until early February 1953. I'm not sure of the exact day when I was moved back from the front; keeping track of the days was neither easy nor important. The circumstances of war are stressful, and we simply performed as trained. Everyone had a duty to fulfill; our safety and survival depended upon supporting and relying on each other.

On that day in early February, a replacement combat medic arrived at the bunker where my sergeant and I spent most of our time. He relieved me of my frontline duties and I was to report to the aid station. There I found a place to sleep, waited for further orders, and assisted with the care of wounded soldiers. These events marked the first steps of my homeward journey. I had reached a turning point and I never again served as an active combat medic. I had survived the frontline and had begun the transition to a long journey home to the US, although not before another deeply sobering incident.

On the first morning away from frontline action I experienced the most devastating blow of all my military experiences. Medics brought my sergeant and replacement medic to the aid station on stretchers. Both were killed in the night. Words cannot express the miserable and anguished feelings I suffered that morning. I had spent several stressful months with the young sergeant. He was a good and skilled soldier. We were a team and he protected me. He provided cover fire to hold the enemy down as I helped wounded soldiers. On dangerous recognizance missions, he knew what to do and our teamwork created a bond. The Korean War escalated to a deep personal level within me as I looked down at him lying on the ground and saw the ultimate sacrifice.

In a flood of confusing thoughts and feelings, my first reaction was to question why and how this had happened. I soon learned that my replacement medic occupied the bunker with the sergeant as another soldier stood guard outside. Unfortunately, the guard soldier fell asleep. A communist soldier killed him first, and then he threw a hand grenade into the bunker killing my sergeant and the medic who replaced me just a few hours earlier. Throughout my service in Korea I had provided care for many wounded and mortally injured soldiers, and my heart went out to all of them. Yet, these two deaths resonated deep within me and I felt completely overwhelmed with emotion. The medic's death was traumatizing because of how quickly it happened to him and how easily it could have been me. The sergeant's death filled me with shocking grief because of the personal bond. I can truly say that I owe my life to this sergeant, but as it turned out, I could not help him make it home alive.

With the backdrop of this awful event, I spent several more days at the aid station. Sometimes it was quiet and there were no wounded soldiers to care for, so we sat around the stove and tried to keep warm. After a couple of calm days, another tragic event occurred.

A US fighter pilot flew over with orders to bomb a target in enemy territory. Regrettably, he dropped the bomb too soon and it landed on some of our men. Devastating casualties accumulated and the combat medics had a lot of work to do that day. As wounded soldiers arrived at the aid station, I assisted with anything I could to relieve the pain and suffering. But even then I struggled with this situation. I soon realized I needed to go out through the trees to take a break from the horrors of war. On that day I saw more blood from these shattered lives than I observed in any of my other experiences; a sight that I still avoid thinking or talking about.

My time at the aid station was brief and intended to be the first step toward home, but it was filled with wrenching experiences that brutally carved out lasting impressions. A person never knew what to expect; we just focused on the situation that confronted us, followed instructions and helped where we could. Soon I was moved from the aid station to another location away from the major hostilities. After this move I began to allow myself to think: "I'm going home. I'm really going home." Step by step, the move away from the Korean War had begun.

Chapter 25
Meeting Paul Fulk

Soon after leaving the aid station I received a letter asking me to find Paul Fulk, a soldier who shared my faith. Either his mother or one of our ministers wrote and asked me to encourage Paul who struggled with the situation in Korea.

Paul also grew up in Illinois, but he lived quite a ways south of me and the distance between our hometowns prevented us from meeting at an earlier time. Being a year younger than me, Paul was drafted into the military as a CO a year after me. He completed his basic training and immediately received orders to go to Korea. The day before he left home, Paul's family received word that a soldier who shared their faith, Donald Borgman, died in Korea. On that sad note, Paul left for Korea without hearing the rest of the story.

After finding Paul's location, I asked a nearby soldier if he knew Paul. He replied, "Yes I do, and that's him standing over there." With a word of thanks, I went and introduced myself to Paul.

Paul had a look of disbelief and surprise. He was still under the impression I died in Korea. He quickly told me what he had heard and was full of questions. I explained that another soldier named Borgman was killed, but the Army notified my parents by mistake.

Our visit was fairly short, yet the connection to home was encouraging. Our fellowship and shared faith strengthened us. It was a brief respite from the stresses of war operations.

Paul asked when we could get together again. I immediately liked this young man and wanted to visit more, but I had to tell him, "I am leaving for the USA tomorrow morning."

I am grateful I met faithful soldiers of our faith while serving in Korea. Those connections sustained me during the difficult hours of the raw realities of war. Paul remembers that our friendship also uplifted and encouraged him.

The visit came at a good time for me, too. It was only a short time prior when I experienced the traumatic events at the aid station after leaving the frontline. I was reminded that there was hope beyond our immediate war situation. Once again I allowed myself to think: "I'm going home. I'm really going home."

Chapter 26
The Journey Home

On February 17, 1953, I received notice that I would begin the long process of returning home; leaving Korea in a few days. February 18th began with a shower in the morning followed by packing my equipment and clothes. A required medical check took place and the captain signed my medical clearance. I got on a truck and went to personnel collecting where I checked in, filled out additional clearance papers and slept there that night. We slept in a tent full of holes, only one stove and almost froze, but no one complained. We were going home.

The next morning, I left via truck for an hour and 45 minute ride to Chunchon. There I boarded the train bound for Yong Dung Po. Walking might have gotten us there faster! At eleven thirty that evening, we finally got off the train and another truck took us to the 45th Replacement Department where, except for a few remaining c-rations, we had our first meal that day. No one complained, however. We were on our way home.

We retired to bed at one in the morning and slept in tents that were only slightly better than accommodations the night previous. A few hours later we were awakened at four thirty and started processing. Even though it was only three and a half hours sleep, no one complained because we were on our way home.

Required medical checks followed the return of all our field equipment, which I sure was happy to part with. After completing forms for forwarding our mail, Army job and civilian occupation, we received awards, decorations, ribbons and medals in the afternoon.

On February 21st, we turned in our sleeping bags and got on trucks that took us to 110th Replacement Company at Inchon, about a 14 mile ride. We turned in two blankets and all our clothes, except for what we wore. More paperwork was filled out, another medical check received, and we patiently waited for a ship to come in. Our accommodations improved remarkably from tents and we now had a building to sleep in.

February 22nd began later in the morning with showers and shaving. That afternoon, we loaded onto trucks and rode across town to the waterfront. Our group remained in the 110th Replacement Depot, and we slept another night in buildings. The Army told us the ship had arrived, but the landing craft had to wait for the tide before it could come to shore to unload and board us. Then a bit later another delay was announced. I didn't understand why. It just seemed like classic Army stuff. So we just waited some more, but we didn't care because we were going home.

February 23rd and 24th consisted of more waiting and February 25th began with another medical check before we continued our wait for departure. We played checkers and dominoes along with other games, and tried to pass the time, but a day was beginning to feel like a year as we waited to go home. The Army ran out of water for us to shower, so we shaved and washed with water we collected from thawing ice. There were 150 of us here when we first arrived, but as our delay dragged on, the number of soldiers grew. Now close to 2,000 men anxiously anticipated their long awaited journey home. Our accommodations were only adequate for about 150 soldiers, but we just crowded in together. February 26th began much the same with more waiting. We played some more games, attempted to pass the time and I pulled an hour of fire guard that evening.

Finally, we received word in the morning of February 27th that we were to get on the landing craft that evening, so we turned in our blankets. At about eight o'clock that evening, we finally marched through the streets of Inchon to the waterfront. We were loaded on a landing craft and taken to our ship, *General Migs,* anchored several miles out in the harbor. Once aboard the ship, we ate supper at about ten thirty that evening. There were 3,800 of us on the ship, a mixed group of US Army, Marines and French Army soldiers.

The next morning I arose early and went on deck. We were quite a ways out to sea, as we had left about an hour earlier. My, what a relief it was to see Korea get smaller and smaller, and finally disappear; a day I looked forward to for a long time.

In the afternoon, I waited in line for four hours at the onboard Postal Exchange (PX) where I bought a camera. I was very excited about my purchase as I began thinking about life back home. It felt like the first tiny step away from a strict military life.

En route to Japan (family photos)

The mood on the ship was much different than when we left San Francisco many months ago. Relief replaced the anxious tension the soldiers felt. Soldiers shared stories as they passed long hours packed together in tight quarters.

I met a man named Richard Corhes. He was friendly and easy to visit with. That first night, Richard and I stayed on deck and talked for a long time. Telling our separate stories and contemplating our futures helped us feel like our Korean experience was being put in the past. Even the weather contributed to that feeling. It got warmer as we sailed south, and it was such a pleasant contrast to the cold Korean winter.

On March 1st, in the morning, we caught a glimpse of the Japanese Islands. At noon we went through the Harbor of Sasabo and soon we docked. Below is a picture of that dock. I was thrilled with my new camera and I looked forward to using it as the journey home unfolded.

Sasabo, Japan dock (family photos)

Getting troops off the boat took a long time. Finally, at about four thirty that afternoon, I got off and climbed onto a bus that took us about four or five miles to Camp Mower. Army officials separated us into groups and my group was taken to the building where we slept and we received orientation from an officer about our processing, camp instructions and other pertinent information.

Everyone felt starved, because we did not get a noon meal on the ship. We waited until about eight thirty that evening when they fed us a special meal that everybody gets upon arriving in Japan from Korea. It consisted of a big steak dinner, including ice cream and milk. It was very good and soon after supper we went to bed. What a wonderful feeling; we actually had a bed with springs and a mattress on it, a pillow, sheets and pillow case. What a luxury! We felt like we'd arrived in a different world. We were almost scared to lie down on the sheet.

While the sheets and bed felt nice, it did not last very long. March 2nd began at one fifteen in the morning when they got us up for processing. We took everything we had with us and went into a big building where we removed our clothes, turned in everything except our shoes and personal belongings, and were carefully searched. Some of the boys still had small weapons in their belongings. They depended on weaponry for so long they did not feel safe without them. I still had a 30 caliber bullet in my pocket that I picked up off the ground and had not yet given to a soldier. I left it in Japan.

Before they issued new clothes, we were run through the showers and given a new issue of underwear, class "A" uniform and fatigues. I felt like a new man getting the Korean dirt off and new clothes on.

At five o'clock that morning, we returned to our barracks to eat breakfast and had a chance to sleep for a couple of hours. Next, a hair cut was required. I waited in line two hours for that before I had a chance to go to the PX. In the evening we had free time, so Richard and I sat down in the snack bar eating cheeseburgers, milkshakes and ice cream sundaes.

On March 3rd we went through personnel processing where we received our pay and got our records straightened out. This took all morning. In the afternoon we were given a two hour presentation explaining why we were sent to Korea, along with an explanation of the GI Bill of Rights. A chaplain spoke for thirty minutes. In the evening, Richard and I went to the snack bar and ate ice cream until we were so full we could hardly walk out.

The next day we had a formation to get a PX ration card. I also placed a request for a telephone call to my parents. The rest of the morning was spent waiting unsuccessfully for the call to go through. In the afternoon I took my Ike jacket (a wool military jacket Gen. Ike Eisenhower liked) to the tailors to have insignias put on and pressed. I was assigned guard duty that afternoon while the rest of the boys received a pass.

On March 5th, I was on guard duty until 4:00pm. When relieved of that obligation, Richard and I went into Sasabo. We had no assignments and we were just waiting for another ship.

I waited in the telephone office again the morning of March 6th until 11:30am when the call to my parents finally went through. This was the first time my parents heard my voice since they received the news I was killed in action.

ᴅonald Borrgman Is Enroute Home From Korean War

Pfc. Donald R. Borgman, son of Mr. and Mrs. Joe Borgman of Baileyville, is enroute home under the Army's rotation program after spending 15 months in Korea with the 45th Inf. Division.

The 45th arrived in Korea in December, 1951, and captured "T-Bone" hill in June's see-saw battle. Pfc. Borgman, a member of Medical Company of the 179th Inf. Regiment, entered the army in April 1951. He received basic training at Fort Meade, Md.

A 1947 graduate of Forreston Community high school, Borgman formerly was a truck driver for Klassy Milling Co., New Glarus, Wis. He holds the Combat Medical badge, UN and Korean servir ribbons and the Korean Presid· tial unit emblem.

On March 7th, one ship was in but I was not to get on that one. Maybe I would get on the next one. I packaged the things I purchased so they would be ready to mail home. In the evening Richard and I got ready and went on pass early to eat supper downtown in Sasabo.

Finally on the morning of March 8th I received my line number for the ship. I knew it wouldn't be long now until I would be leaving. I filled out five changes of address cards and mailed my box home. I went to the snack bar for more ice cream before I began guard duty at six o'clock that evening and throughout the next 24 hours. On March 9th I was assigned to guard duty all day. That evening I went to the snack bar and service club.

Much to my disappointment, on the morning of March 10th, they told us all orders were changed, and we would not leave yet for another few days. So the next several days were spent much the same: sleeping in late, getting passes to Sasabo, going to the service club to play games, and eating meals at the snack bar.

Finally on March 15th, at one o'clock in the afternoon we again obtained a line number for the ship. We received another medical check, took three pills, a clothing check, customs declaration forms and a shake down. We turned in our bedding and after supper we waited around a little while before they loaded us on semi-trailers and buses to take us down to the ship. We boarded the ship at about 10 o'clock that night.

I do not have a day by day account of the voyage from Japan to Seattle, but I remember working in the mess hall. I also remember being sick again on the first part of the journey. After several days on the water, one thing remains vividly clear in my mind towards the end of the trip: we could begin to see the top of the Canadian Mountains, and we knew we were getting close to good old USA. There were about four or five thousand happy soldiers on that ship as we moved closer to the dock in Seattle.

Below is a picture of the Seattle waterfront with the "Welcome Home" sign. The band played for us as we neared the dock.

Seattle dock (family photo)

Fathers, mothers, wives, sisters, brothers and grandparents waited with tears in their eyes as they welcomed us soldiers home to good old USA. My parents chose not to drive to Seattle because I did not have time to spend with them at that point.

From the dock in Seattle, the Army provided bus transportation to the military barracks at Fort Lawton. Further arrangements via train took me to Fort Carson, CO and finally I arrived back home in Illinois. Many times in more recent years, my wife Joann and have I visited our family in Seattle where we like to enjoy breakfast at the Space Needle. From there, I look down to see the dock where I stepped off of the ship and had my first step back on American soil.

At Home

Chapter 27
Arriving Home

My time at Fort Carson, CO was brief. This is where the Army paid back-pay since the time I was reported killed in action. I was also given the extra pay earned from being under enemy fire from October, 1952 until sometime in February, 1953. The Army also provided train fare from Fort Carson to Sterling, IL as I inched along my journey home.

'Dead' GI Home

Pfc. Donald Borgman, who was reported killed in action Nov. 5, returned from Korea to his home in Baileyville this week, very much alive. He is the son of Mr. and Mrs. Joe Borgman.

GI Officially Dead, Returns Home Unhurt

(Consolidated News Service)

BAILEYVILLE — A Korean veteran from Baileyville who was reported killed in action last Nov. 5 has arrived home, very much alive.

He is Pfc. Donald Borgman, only child of Mr. and Mrs. Joe Borgman, Baileyville.

Borgman himself did not realize he was officially dead until he tried to collect his pay last Dec. 1. He was informed his name had been removed from the payroll.

Several days later he received a letter from home explaining that the defense department had reported him killed in action, even though letters he wrote after Nov. 5 had arrived in Baileyville. The defense department claimed the error resulted when a William Borgman in a nearby rifle company was killed Nov. 5.

"The way things worked out, the news I had been reported killed in action didn't come as much of a shock," Borgman said calmly.

His parents, however, suffered the ordeal of first believing their only child had been killed, but learning several days later he was really safe.

The number 5 has been an important figure in Borgman's service career. He left home to enter the army April 5, 1951, arrived at Camp Stoneman, Cal., for overseas shipment Oct. 5, 1951, and arrived in Yokohama, Japan, Nov. 5, 1951. He was reported killed in action Nov. 5, 1952, and arrived home safely Easter Sunday, April 5.

I arrived in Illinois on a Sunday morning and was greeted by my father, mother, Aunt Dena and Don Myers. At long last, I was home.

Mother and me at home (family photo)

This picture of my mother and me was taken upon my return; my parent's home is in the background. The picture is interesting because it marks the end of my first Korean journey after I returned home safely. Yet, the picture also marks the beginning of my second Korean journey; a much longer journey of coming to terms with my war experiences.

The picture contains a great deal of meaning that seems expressive and fitting. At the beginning of this book I am pictured on a similar porch with my dog and great buddy, Fritzie. Now the house is in the distance. I was feeling a bit distant, too. There were experiences I could not talk about, and feelings I didn't understand. The expressions in this picture depict the second journey I needed to travel. My mother was beaming with joy, because I was home safe and alive. My expression is more uncertain. I needed to bridge the differences behind the expressions and it would take years.

The military asked me to report on Monday morning to the draft board in Freeport, IL to let them know I had returned home. I reported as requested and received my honorable discharge certificate.

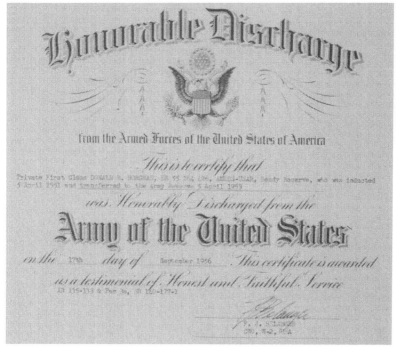

Honorable Discharge Certificate

Once that was finished, the Army asked if I would consider representing the United States Army at a funeral in Freeport the next day for a soldier killed in Korea. I accepted the request and agreed to attend. This was a request, not a command, because as of this day I was a veteran, not a soldier. I dressed in my class "A" uniform again and I wore it to the funeral. It was not easy!

While I was happy to represent the United States Army, it was very difficult to see all the tears and sobs from mother, father, and the rest of the family and friends for one who gave his young life for his country. When two soldiers are in combat, it is impossible to know why one soldier comes home unhurt and the other soldier loses his life.

For me, the hardest part of the service was realized when the bugler played *Taps*. It is a simple tune, yet emotionally stirring. Some of my war experiences traumatized my sensibilities and left buried anxieties. I didn't understand the feelings or know how to think about them. The single bugle playing *Taps* for a fallen soldier reached deep inside me, somehow brushed up against those feelings, and I felt very sad. *Taps* began with three notes and a rhythm that called to attention. The tempo then quickened and the music became anxious. A climax was quickly reached and then the music began to drift down into the distance. *Taps* ended as it began, but the three notes were faded and wistful. Then all was silent among the small gathered group. A breeze stirred through the somber moment. What was known and loved about the fallen soldier was confined to memories. The price had been paid.

Memories came flooding in of the sergeant and the medic who replaced me on the frontline. I was fortunate to be home. They lost their life. As I reflected back on this situation and the power of the music to stir those feelings, I became curious about the origin of *Taps*. There are several different accounts, but the exact origins are simply not known. The account that seems most fitting dates back to the Civil War.

It all began in 1862 during the Civil War when Union Army Captain Robert Ellicombe, was with his men near Harrison's Landing in Virginia. The Confederate Army was on the other side of the narrow strip of land. During the night, Captain Ellicombe heard the moans of a soldier who lay severely wounded on the field. Not knowing if it was a Union or Confederate soldier, the captain decided to risk his life and bring the stricken man back for medical attention.

Crawling on his stomach through the gunfire, the captain reached the stricken soldier and began pulling him toward his encampment. When the captain finally reached his own lines, he discovered it was actually a Confederate soldier, but the soldier was dead. The Captain lit a lantern and suddenly caught his breath and went numb with shock. In the dim light, he saw the face of the soldier. It was his son.

The boy had been studying music in the South when the war broke out. Without telling his father, the boy enlisted in the Confederate Army. The following morning, heartbroken, the father asked permission of his superiors to give his son a full military burial despite his enemy status. His request was only partially granted. The captain had asked if he could have a group of Army band members play a funeral dirge for his son at the funeral. The request was turned down since the soldier was Confederate. But out of respect for the father, they did say they could give him one musician. The captain chose a bugler. He asked the bugler to play a series of musical notes he had found on a piece of paper in the pocket of the dead youth's uniform. This wish was granted. The haunting melody, we now know as "Taps" used at military funerals, was born. (Camp White Military Museum)

In a short while, the tragic brutality of war touched our extended family too. My cousin, Robert Kappenman, entered the Army in December, 1952. He was sent to Korea in July, 1953. He served in the 45th Infantry, the same as me. I never had the opportunity to meet Robert, and unfortunately he was killed in Korea sometime after I returned home.

Chapter 28
Telling About My Korean Experience

After arriving home I quickly became busy with my American life. There were other responsibilities; my career, my family and friends. I did not really take time to contemplate my Korean War experience and what it meant to me. Nor did I talk about it much. Frankly, it was too hard to talk about; especially in front of a group of people. It was so uncomfortable reaching into the traumatized emotions and sensibilities. I felt that part of my life was deeply misunderstood, because I did not know how to adequately relate the experience. Yet, it was an enormous part of my young adult life. The war could not just be forgotten and buried in the past. Over time, life's experiences helped me understand the value of my Korean War service.

The first thing I faced upon returning home from Korea was finding and living with adjustment. I really do not have the words to describe this unavoidable process. Only another veteran has any knowledge of what this adjustment process is all about. When I reflect on my own adjustment back to civilian life, I remember needing something to occupy my mind; something that provided vision and direction for life in general. Though I didn't realize it while I was going through the process, I was experiencing restlessness; something that I didn't have prior to going to Korea. So, first I bought a new car. Not that I needed a new car, but I wanted a change; something new. Next, I bought a Harley Davidson motorcycle; something I really enjoyed.

Soon it was time to find employment and establish a career. That became a simple and easy problem to resolve. A distant relative of my mother was a home builder and offered me a job as well as training for home building. I was very well accepted within the construction company; both from the owner and other employees because of my military service. This was the beginning of my building career that continued for 55 years.

Traveling was another way in which I tried to adjust to "normal" life. Besides local travel, I also went to Florida, Canada, Wisconsin, and even to Mexico with my good buddy and cousin, Don Myers. Now when I look back on that period of time, I feel that I was looking for something to help erase the trauma of war, but I did not understand my need very well.

I was living at home with my parents at this time. As I think of that now, I realize how my parents would have had a very difficult time trying to understand my "adjustment period." They had no knowledge of what I had done or seen on the frontlines, nor the conditions under which I was functioning. I do not remember telling them anything about my experiences in Korea; we simply were not encouraged to talk about it. So, the past was not something I spent much time thinking about, when I could help it. Rather, the future was my goal now that I was home.

Though I found ways to be occupied most of the time with all this activity, I am certain that I was still very unsettled. Don and I decided to travel down to Mexico for a vacation. His father offered his new Buick for the trip, and that was great. After seeing the bullfights in Mexico City, we traveled further south with Guatemala in our thoughts. But we changed our minds when we realized that the terrain was rough, and that food and gas supplies in general could quickly become a concern. In retrospect, bullfights and travelling into possible physical danger was probably not a great idea for a recovering traumatized soldier. We decided to head to the ocean for a swim on our way back up north to California. Soon we met a man who spoke a bit of English, and he tried to tell us, "Sharks, sharks." So that ended the swimming party.

I also traveled through Canada a bit. On one of my drives to Canada, I chauffeured a couple in their car. I had to get a train back to Chicago once we reached our destination. Don and his girlfriend met me at the Chicago train station, and she proceeded to tell me about a new girl in town. She thought it may be someone I might like. It sounded like the girl was attractive and nice to be with. Sunday morning the three of us went to our fellowship meeting and the new girl was there. It was Joann Justus! Joann and I had our first day together which led to our marriage in 1955.

With time, things did start to settle down as I resumed "normal" civilian life. Still there were events that took place that helped me realize a need to have other things to do and concentrate on when I was trying to escape the terror of war. Joann understood this too and offered suggestions. After two of our children were born, Joann encouraged me to take up flying lessons. I did well with both the written test and the pilot training. The flight test instructor even told me I should consider further training for more advanced areas in that field.

Flying provided a fun and interesting hobby for many years, but it did not become my career. Yet, I learned that "escape" would not work well for me: I needed to find a way to really come to terms with the reason for my Korean War service.

Periodically I would mull over my Korean experiences and wonder why it had to happen. Over time I learned about various Korean events and wondered if it was the purpose for the war. The answer began to take shape as I heard more about Korean people accepting the gospel. The Korean people needed help resisting a takeover by communists and the repression it would bring. Freedom in South Korea has brought many opportunities that they have used very well. I began to understand the complex and subtle value of helping a people even when the help is very costly.

Chapter 29
Deciding to Return to Korea

Joann has always shown an interest in my military experience. Her interest brought me joy as she inquired about Korea and looked forward to seeing ministers come back from Korea with stories of the gospel and its acceptance in Korea. Again in retrospect, I now realize I was looking for ways to appropriately remember and share my experiences in Korea; it remained a very difficult challenge to balance the memories and the horror.

It wasn't very long before we received invitations to visit Korea. It was very encouraging for me to hear about the gospel in Korea, and to realize how the Korean people had begun to accept it. Further, I was encouraged to hear that the poor people I had seen and lived with in 1951 – 1953 were free from communism and starvation. Now they had roads, cars, food to eat and shelter, but most of all they had freedom.

In 1990, Joann and I made plans to go to Korea. This was 37 years after I walked down the boat ramp in Seattle with the band playing on the dock to welcome us home. During those 37 years I had many thoughts about my Korean experiences and wondered, "What does Korea look like now?" I would soon see what the Korean people accomplished with their tremendous opportunity. Merlin Howlet, Paul Boyd and Ann Bailor were three ministers who continually invited us back to Korea, "Come to Korea; we want you to see it now."

The Korean government offered veterans a trip back to visit Korea. Though I appreciated the offer and the demonstration of their thankfulness for Korean War veterans, I did not accept the travel packaged planned by the government. Rather, I wanted to be with Koreans in their homes enjoying fellowship and rice together. I wanted to hear the stories of our friends, and hear their own personal feelings about what the US involvement had made possible in Korea. But most importantly, I wanted to see Koreans enjoying the gospel and what it has brought to them.

Though I really wanted to go back to Korea, another voice would come and say, "Do you really want to go back to that place?" Many veterans did not share the positive perspectives that I was learning. I remember waiting in a lobby for an oil change one time and the man sitting beside me began to talk. He was a Korean veteran too and the subject soon turned to the war. I told him that my wife and I were going back to Korea, and that she wanted to see the country where I had spent my military time. He became very upset and I feared that he might lose control right there in the waiting room. I felt sorry for that man, because he failed to see the benefits of the Korean War. That visit ended quickly and I was again thankful for a growing insight into the value of helping a people in desperate need. It is hard for me to see why men like him cannot understand the value of freedom and opportunity as a result of the war.

*Joann, Diane and me at the airport in Seattle when Joann and I left
for Korea, 1990 (family photo)*

*Boeing 747 leaving Seattle for Korea with Joann and me onboard,
1990 (family photo)*

Conclusion

Chapter 30
I Love Korea

Visiting Korea with Joann in 1990 was an invaluable experience. Immediately impressive was the progress South Korea realized in the 40 years since the war. Of course I had followed Korea's economic growth and development over the years, but seeing it firsthand and experiencing it was much more meaningful. What has been developed is especially noticeable when North and South Korea are compared. At the end of the war an armistice established the demilitarized zone (DMZ) separating North and South Korea. Visiting the DMZ confirms a vast contrast. However, the war was not just about economic prosperity and creating distinctions and contrasts. The war was simply about freedom. Freedom has brought many positive outcomes, and I am confident that it was all very worth it. I value my opportunity of participating in this great fight for freedom.

Earlier in this book, I referenced two questions, "Why are we here?" and "What are we fighting for?" Generals MacArthur and Ridgway had very good and reasonable answers to both of the questions; yet there is even more. Koreans have prospered and their freedom has allowed them to enjoy a rich and open fellowship. As result of my visit to Korea, I was able to feel a connection to the people and better understand the far reaching effects of helping them during the war. It took many years and a return trip to Korea with Joann by my side before I fully comprehended the depth in the answers to those two questions. Today I am very thankful that the answers I received while visiting Korea in 1990 are much richer and more rewarding than the ones we were given in 1950.

Over and over again Korean people displayed their genuine happiness about meeting a Korean War veteran from the United States. These people continue to appreciate the help we provided. Meeting people in Korea helped me develop a whole new positive perspective; a precious connection to the people. Meeting our ministers and people of our faith was especially helpful and added depth to my understanding. Hearing about many people receiving the gospel is one thing, but being with the people created a far richer relationship. As we attended our church convention, I experienced an invaluable appreciation for the Korean people.

Joann and I sat close to the front during the convention. One of the ministers began the first convention meeting by requesting we sing a hymn. I knew the tune, but not the Korean words; I just wept. I was not able to control myself. I had overwhelming feelings and emotion knowing that US soldiers had a little part in making convention possible in Korea. No longer do I need to wonder why we were there and what we fought for in 1950.

We have wonderful privileges in our generation because we have opportunities of seeing the effects of God's work. It is a wonderful thing to think of God seeing people as individuals before Him, and providing for peoples' individual needs. Knowing God's care for his people has helped me to better appreciate my participation in helping a nation of people in need. My horizons are enlarged in a way that no other experience could provide. It is my wish that every Korean Veteran could return to Korea for an experience similar to mine.

Looking back, I now realize that my Korean War experience consists of two journeys. The first journey, my military experience, ended when I arrived home safely. The second journey, coming to terms with the reasons for my Korean War experience, has come to a very positive conclusion. The emotions still run very deep and it can still be difficult to openly talk about everything that happened. But the difficulty of finding adequate language in spite of my emotions does not diminish the positive feelings I have about what was accomplished.

In Japan, 1952 (family photo)

The above picture in my class "A" uniform was taken in Japan on my return trip home from Korea. The uniform is still hanging in my closet. Occasionally, I remove it to take a good look at it. However, I quickly return it to the closet before the tears start to come. With the occasional momentary flashback of what I saw and participated in during the war, I have to stop to remind myself that I really am safely home, and the outcome has been for the good of countless people. The cost was high for many, but we had a part in stopping communism and tyranny from spreading to another part of the world. I know many US Korean War veterans who share great joy knowing we had a part in preserving freedom; creating an opportunity for the gospel to enjoy open fellowship in South Korea. Our joy is increased as we realize many Korean ministers are leaving their country to take the gospel to other parts of the world.

One Wednesday night we attended a bible study in a Korean home. We sat around the room on the floor; the Korean custom. After the meeting, Dick Owen explained to our friends that I had served in the military during the Korean War. A young girl was listening very closely to every word that was being said. She lived in the home where we met. When Dick finished the story this girl got up, left the room, and quickly returned. She handed me a notebook and pen and said, "Sign." With tears in my eyes I signed her tablet. That experience alone answered the question why we fought the Korean War, and explained for me what we fought for. It was obvious to me that the story was being kept alive. This young girl had been told about the war and how other countries had helped them. She had some understanding of the costs associated with freedom, and she was grateful.

The home of Wednesday night meeting (family photo)

During the war I began a connection with the Korean people; especially during my countryside walks around 121 Evac. Visiting Korea again renewed that connection in a special way. Now it is clearer than ever that the simple decency of respectful human interaction transcends the bluster, brutality and madness of war. My 1990 visit to Korea made the benefits of the war much more obvious. As it turns out, this is really a story about people helping people. I spent time helping the Korean people in their time of need. My time of need developed in-between the war and my return visit to Korea. I needed to better understand the purpose in my experience. Seeing what the Korean people have done with their freedom and opportunities, as well as seeing the gospel reach out to so many was a tremendous help. The Korean people have helped me!

Epilogue

There are a few items beyond my Korean War experience that add additional perspective. It is included here if you are interested, but it is in no particular order.

Visiting Korea

Chapter 31
Returning to Korea

Our flight from Seattle continued north over the Aleutian Islands and along the coast of Russia to Korea. We landed at Seoul International Airport. I had been to this airport a few times during the war, but as soldiers we called it an airstrip. I knew it would be large and modern, yet the contrast from what I remembered made quite an impression. I would experience this feeling many times as Joann and I toured and I rediscovered Korea. What a difference 50 years of freedom made. The picture below is further illustration of the economic progress. This was a war devastated area in 1952 and now it is thriving.

Korean city thriving with freedom, 1990 (family photo)

Seoul, Korea 1990 (family photo)

Hotel we stayed at our first night in Korea, 1990 (family post card)

We were met at the airport by Merlin Howlett, a minister from Canada who labored many years in Korea. He took us to a luxurious hotel; another representation of the economic progress Korea had made since the war. Getting a good rest helped us adjust to the time zone, and gave me a chance to reflect on the fact that I was once again back in Korea. It was exciting, yet I felt a little anxious. What would it be like to visit some of the key sites of my war experience?

Artillery being fired from jeeps (Song, p. 13, 10)

The above photos show artillery mounted on a jeep in action. This was a very typical sight of the frontlines. We spent many months observing this very activity and it remains a permanent impression as I reflected back and remembered what Korea was like. The last part of my war experience was traumatic and filled with shocking situations. Everything you can imagine about a war's frontline and more. Yet, what kept coming to mind was the countryside walks around 121 Evac and meeting ordinary Korean people. It was exciting to meet Korean people again and see what they had accomplished with their freedom. Traumatic memories would be triggered, but this time they would not dominate. Those memories have their legitimate place, yet being with thankful and respectful Korean people was far more powerful.

Much of our travel in Korea was kindly planned by the ministers from Korea, the US, Canada and other countries. They knew what a veteran should do and see in Korea. Their planning made our visit possible and memorable. I will always be grateful for what was done for us. We only spent one night at the first hotel before traveling on to the convention grounds where Koreans and ministers of our faith were gathered. It was a tremendous beginning for a fresh new connection to Korea.

The convention was truly the highlight of our Korean trip. The next two pictures are of the meeting tent; the first one is the speaking platform, and the second picture is Joann in the area where we sat.

Speaking platform and Joann at the Korean convention (family photo)

Don Garland, Korean convention (family photo)

Don Garland, one of our ministers, was a great help to me many times throughout my experiences. It was a thrill to be at the Korean convention with him. I first met Don in Japan where he helped me buy a set of dishes for my mother. Through the years he was a constant and positive connection to Korea. He and a few other Korean ministers visited us when we lived in Illinois.

Our last visit together was a few years after this picture when he visited us in Colorado. Don came for the convention at Hotchkiss and spent a night in our home. The next day when we took him to the airport and said our parting goodbyes, I had a strong feeling it might be the last time we would see him. He passed away a few years later, but his memory will continue to live on with us.

One summer day in 1952 two young Korean boys taught me to remove my shoes when entering a Korean building. The custom lives on and is just as important today. It is simply clean and respectful. Below is a picture of the shoe rack inside the convention meeting area.

Shoe rack at Korean convention (family photo)

Joann and I stayed on the convention grounds. I slept in the men's quarters and Joann was with the Korean woman. Joann is pictured here with four Korean women in their sleeping quarters. She really enjoyed being with the ladies, but language was a little problem. They tried so hard to understand each other.

Joann with Korean ladies, their names below, Korean convention (family photo)

Everyone truly made Joann and I feel like special guests. I love rice and I am very fond of the way Koreans prepare it with kimchi. When the Korean ministers learned this, they made sure that I had plenty of rice to eat at each meal. The food was delicious. In the picture below you will also notice many children. I loved seeing all the Korean children and thinking about how they can enjoy freedom. It was truly satisfying seeing them and knowing that I had a small part in contributing to their freedom and stopping the atrocities that their parents and grandparents endured.

Children and mealtime at Korean convention (family photos)

Korean convention (family photo)

It was fun watching them organize a picture of all the children. I love to think of their opportunities growing up as faithful adults in a free land. They are the hope of the future. For me it was uplifting and encouraging.

Later in the day, a group of the older Korean children sang together. It was inspiring to see young people upholding the way and standards of the Bible.

Korean convention (family photo)

These two pictures represent an important part of coming to terms with my Korean War experience. Seeing them allowed me to realize the hope and opportunity provided for these children. I had a part in allowing them the chance to sing the *Songs of Zion*. It gave meaning to all the efforts of keeping the tyranny associated with the North Korean communists from taking over South Korea. Thinking of this stirs deep emotion. The war was awful in so many ways, but seeing what has been accomplished with freedom is deeply satisfying. It was worth it.

Korean convention (family photo)

The ministers who attended the 1990 Korean convention are pictured above. Jinju Kim, the fifth person in the third row was at our home one time for a Sunday morning fellowship meeting when we lived in Illinois.

Korean convention (family photo)

The photo above illustrates the traditional Korean dress. There are many cultural differences and it would be easy to think that this would cause division. Instead, what I experienced was unity. Unity in faith had much to do with it, but there was also obvious recognition for an individual soldier who played a small part in securing their freedom. This brought unity as well.

Another time when I was walking down the street of Seoul, a schoolboy standing on the side of the street bowed to me as I passed. He would have perhaps known by my age and nationality that there was a good chance I had fought for their country. There is an overwhelming awareness among the Korean people that the Americans came to help fight for freedom. Again and again my return visit to Korea made it easier and easier for me to know why I was there during the war. I felt so honored, and all the credit goes to Korean people. It is phenomenal what they have accomplished with their freedom and the way they respect and honor returning veterans.

Sproulie Denio's grave (family photo)

I was grateful for the opportunity to visit Sproulie's grave. He told me many years ago that Korea would be the springboard for the gospel in Asia. Now to be able to visit Korea today, to attend a convention and observe the gospel being sent forth to other countries by Korean ministers is truly a miracle that I am grateful to be a part of. Sproulie said the war was absolutely necessary; veterans who have returned to visit Korea can easily see that to be true.

Another minister on the Korean staff, Dick Owen, was our tour guide for several days. He is a longtime friend of our family and also a Korean War Veteran. He served after me, and assisted in the cleanup efforts after the war.

With Dick's help, Joann and I had the privilege of attending a funeral for a Korean of our faith. The Korean burial customs were interesting. All of us were transported by bus out to the countryside; the burial site. In addition to Dick, there were eight Korean ministers. The bus had a low compartment to hold the casket during transport. Added to intrigue of the procession was the weather; heavy rains caused muddy roads and the bus got stuck.

The sons of the deceased woman were dressed in mourning garments. They removed the casket from the funeral bus and carried it down a long path to the burial site. The casket was covered with a gold cloth which was removed at the grave.

Korean funeral (family photo)

After the service, another cloth was spread over a little rise in the field and a luncheon was served. Joann and I were graciously invited to join them though we questioned whether or not we should. Dick and Koreans generously encouraged us to partake. We greatly appreciated how the Koreans included us during a deeply personal time.

After lunch we walked back out to the road where our bus was waiting. Two of the women ministers invited us for tea back at the batch where they lived. Our time with them was truly enjoyable.

Women ministers' batch with Dick Owen left of center (family photo)

After tea, Dick asked me to tell the story of faith in our family. With Dick as my interpreter, I began my story. I was not accustomed to speaking through an interpreter, but I did the best I could. I started by telling about my Grandmother Borgmann reading the German bible (I still have that bible). She read about Jesus establishing a ministry of two going together without homes of their own, and how they traveled from one place to another speaking the gospel that Jesus brought to the world. She searched for these ministers and told her family about them, but unfortunately she passed away before they came to northern Illinois. However, her children recognized what she had described when ministers arrived with the gospel.

Dick encouraged me by relating how much my story meant to the young Korean ministers. They didn't have any stories like that in Korea because the first ministers had not been there very long at that time. It is interesting how telling one's story deepens friendships and connections that could otherwise be lost to language barriers.

Later, Dick took Joann and me to visit a Buddhist Temple. It reminded me of the time during the war when two boys who were hiking with me. This time I remembered to take off my shoes! As we observed the intricate structures inside the temple, I could not help but wonder what became of the two boys.

Buddhist temple (family photo)

In the photo below, Joann, Dick and I are in a Korean home of some of our friends. Take notice how low the table is to the floor. Can you imagine me trying to get my long legs under the table? As I said before, I love Korean food. This picture shows why I wanted to go to Korea on my own expense rather than the government sponsored tour. I wanted to be in Korean homes and I wanted to hear their stories. Just look at the rice and good food! It would be impossible for anyone to show more respect than these people showed Joann and me. They said, "Thank you," over and over again for what the US did during the war.

Meal in a Korean home (family photo)

One afternoon, Ann Bailor took Joann and me on a hike up in the mountains. Again, I was reminded of the mountainous terrain where I carried wounded soldiers away from the frontline. This time was different, however. We could leisurely enjoy the scenery and observe the numerous small temples along the trail. It was an interesting time and provided a glimpse of historic Korean culture as well as a view of the beautiful Korean landscape.

Joann and me hiking the hillside (family photo)

We also met a young family that lived on a convention grounds. I was delighted that I had the opportunity to meet and visit with this family and know that they have the same freedom as we have in America.

Korean family at convention (family photo)

Looking at these pictures is not the same as meeting and visiting with the people, but hopefully these photos will help all of us understand what the war accomplished. Hopefully reading this will convey the magnitude of the gift of hope and opportunity that Koreans have grasped.

Chapter 32
Korea's Demilitarized Zone

During our 1990 Korean visit, Ann Bailor took a group of us north to the Demilitarized Zone (DMZ) at Panmunjom where formal diplomatic discussions were held. We were allowed inside the building where peace talks took place between the Communist North Korea, South Korea and the United States.

United Nations on the left and the North Koreans on the right, 1952
(Post Card)

We also visited the *Bridge of No Return*. This old bridge stretches across a river that now forms the border between North and South Korea. When Joann and I were walking around the area we looked across the line between South and North Korea and saw the communist soldiers watching us through binoculars.

Bridge of No Return, 1990 (Post Card)

This picture shows the *Bridge of No Return* and the Poplar tree where two United Nations commanding officers were murdered by the North Koreans in 1976.

North Korea, 1990 (Post Card)

This photo is looking north into North Korea. The *Bridge of No Return* is just beyond the larger tree in the middle.

North Korean "building", 1990 (family photo)

We were told that there is nothing on the other side of the building in this picture. It is simply just another façade, or propaganda of communism. Apparently it was built to impress the visitors of Panmunjom.

The tour of the area also took us down to one of the tunnels that the communist dug with the thought of finding a way to capture South Korea. When we reached the dividing line at the bottom of the tunnel, there was a communist soldier; he looked very sad. We wished he could one day enjoy freedom.

Chapter 33
Outpouring of Korean Gratitude

Many Koreans remember the war and are very thankful. Even young people are thankful for Korea War veterans. A statute of Douglas MacArthur was one way of paying tribute to what the US did in securing freedom for Korea.

Left - MacArthur memorial, 1990
Right - Children at MacArthur memorial, 1990 (family photos)

A group of school children were on a fieldtrip visiting the Douglas MacArthur memorial when Joann and I were there. Though they couldn't speak much English, and we spoke no Korean, it was obvious the children have been taught to express their gratitude for freedom and what the US did to ensure their freedom. The student between Joann and me kept saying, "Thank you, thank you," in English. The others were all smiles, too, also saying, "Thank you," in Korean. Another time an older lady came up to us, a stranger in the street, and with tears in her eyes managed to express her gratitude. Again, this travel experience put reason behind our war efforts.

An afternoon was spent with our longtime friend, Dick Owen, walking and enjoying our time in a park.   We met a group of women singing Korean songs accompanied with music from their Korean instruments.   Dick greeted them and they immediately asked if I was a Korean War veteran. When Dick responded that I was, the women were overjoyed and insisted that he and I play their instruments with them.

In a park with Dick Own, 1990 (family photo)

On another occasion, a complete stranger approached Dick and asked if I was a Korean War veteran. Dick told the man a little of my experience and service during the war. The man offered to take us anywhere we wanted to visit in his own personal car; something certainly new for Koreans because there were practically no cars during the war.

All three of us were very impressed and thankful for this man's expression of gratitude. I indicated I would like to see the place at Inchon where I ran ashore that cold night in 1951. The man readily agreed and was happy to transport us the 40 miles. When we arrived, the man gave us a brief tour of a war memorial. He soon ran short of time, so we thanked him for his generosity and told him we would make other arrangements for our return.

The generous man, me and Dick Owen, 1990 (family photo)

Now back in Inchon, I wanted to see the harbor again. However, it was something I needed to do alone and did not want anyone else with me. I did not go right up to the water's edge; rather I stayed back a ways to observe a panoramic view of the harbor. It was then that I lost all my composure. Raw emotions poured out as the memories flooded back. It was difficult comprehending what had happened to me that night long ago when I went ashore and found myself in a country torn apart by an enemy who wanted total control. Again, I do not know how to express the thoughts and emotions I experienced that day. I suspect only another veteran will truly understand my feelings.

After a short while, Joann came and put her arms around me. Then I was able to return to the present day and once again gain control of my emotions. It was actually a good experience. It was good to see Inchon again with my growing understanding of the purpose for the war and the many positive things it made possible. After spending a little more time at the memorial, we left to make arrangements for our return trip to Seoul. Before leaving we also visited an elderly Korean lady, one of our friends, in an Inchon hospital.

Joann supporting at Inchon, 1990 (family photo)

We returned to Seoul on a bus where we visited the United Nations Plaza. Flags representing all the nations that participated in the Korean War are flown in honor of their contribution.

United Nations Plaza, 1990 (family photo)

United Nations Troop Strength

- Republic of Korea   590,911
- Columbia   1,068
- United States   302,483
- Belgium   900
- United Kingdom   14,198
- South Africa   826
- Canada   6,146
- The Netherlands   819
- Turkey   5,453
- Luxembourg   44
- Australia   2,282
- Philippines   1,496
- New Zealand   1,385
- Thailand   1,204
- Ethiopia   1,271
- Greece   1,263
- France   1,119

(Korean War, para 13)

Chapter 34
I'm Happy We Returned to Visit Korea

While flying home from Korea, I had time to reflect on what I learned during my visit and think about my new feelings. I felt a renewed and strengthened connection to the Korean people. I particularly enjoyed thinking about the children at the convention and all the other thousands of children who are growing up in freedom; living in comfortable homes, enjoying the same freedom I enjoy in America.

Yes, I love being a Korean War veteran. Just to think that I had a little part in obtaining the freedom that these people and their children can enjoy. I know now what we were fighting for. If I ever forget or yet again question why we were at war in Korea, all I need to do is take out the picture of the little girl with her parents at convention. It will bring tears to my eyes again and remind me that I love Korea and I know why I was there.

Our flight back to Seattle was very interesting on another packed Boeing 747. Once airborne, Joann and I heard crying coming from the rear of the plane. We wondered why. It did not let up, but continued and seemed to increase. So Joann and I went to investigate. We found two young women with the colossal responsibility of caring for Korean babies who were en route to Seattle for adoption. Joann and I asked the women if we could help them. They responded, "Oh please!" We each took a baby and started to walk up and down the aisles. We continued doing this with several of the babies and were grateful for the size of the aircraft! The picture shows that an old combat medic can take care of babies as well.

Return flight to Seattle (family photo)

Our daughter, Diane, greeted us when we returned to Seattle. It was obvious to her that our Korean visit was a tremendously positive experience.

Diane, Joann and me in Seattle (family photo)

Korean War Service Remembered

Chapter 35
Korean War Memorial in Washington DC

In Washington DC there is a fitting memorial for the Korean War. It is a field of soldiers trudging forward in seemingly bleak conditions. It represents well the human element of the war. I appreciate that it does not glamorize the war, yet it in no way diminishes the necessity and benefit of the war. It is a nice balance of respect, solemnness and portrayal of willingness to help a nation in need.

Korean Veteran's Memorial, Washington, D.C. (family photos)

As a veteran, life at war was a part of our lives that we remember as both the best and the worst times. It was a time when life was lived in unexplainable conditions, where the highs and adventures came equally shared with heavy burdens, hardship, tragedy and loss. It was during this time of fighting that we as young men were stretched to the limits of our courage, fears, strength and endurance. It was a bazaar mix of shock, tedium and camaraderie. Technology at that time wasn't advanced like it is today; we experienced close combat with readily defined frontlines. Vigilance was paramount.

I am happy that I have been able to write about my experiences. It was a great day when we arrived back in the good, old USA. Those of us who served in the defense of this nation know all too well what it means to respond to a threat to the freedom of a people.

Our history demonstrates that freedom has never been easy. It has always required vigilance, sacrifice and war, to preserve what we value about this nation. War is such a messy business, and there are many who want no part of it. This is understandable, but not altogether realistic. All it takes for evil to succeed in the world is for good people to stand back and do nothing.

When I see a man in uniform today or a veteran with his cap on, I walk up to him and say, "Thanks for serving," and tell them I am a Korean War veteran. We may both shed some tears; maybe can't even speak, but we are proud Americans!

I am grateful for memorials. They are a place where a person from any background can pause, take notice and consider for a moment what has been done; what price has been paid. Memorials are a piece of the fabric of remembering the story.

Chapter 36
Veteran Reunion

I enjoyed the Korean War Veteran's Reunion in 2006; the first one I attended. Though I wasn't comfortable sharing my own personal experiences in front of 500 people, I appreciated all that the others shared. I appreciated hearing directly from other soldiers and the Koreans themselves. It had been 54 years since I returned home from Korea.

One brief account was from a veteran who told us he arrived in Korea during the war. He did not say where in Korea, but a location nearby a train. From a distance, he thought the flat train cars were loaded with railroad ties. But as he neared the train, he realized it had been loaded with frozen bodies. They were stacked four or five feet high. This man could see the rings on some of the fingers indicating they were probably married. It was a terrible experience for this solder who himself had only been married about a month. He made it back home safely and he mustered the courage to share his story.

We heard many fascinating and dreadful stories of some of the Koreans who escaped the communists of North Korea. We also heard many personal accounts and tributes from veterans. It was helpful and interesting to hear and consider all the perspectives. Perhaps with this book I can offer a helpful contribution.

Chapter 37
Reconnecting with Paul Fulk

Joann and I moved from Illinois to Colorado in 1990. Through some mutual friends, Norman and Annebelle Britz, Paul Fulk had received my new telephone number. Soon after, I received a phone call one afternoon. Joann answered the phone and brought it to me saying, "Somebody wants to talk to you." When I said hello, the person responded, "This is Paul Fulk." I hadn't remembered that name, nor did I remember the visit we had together in Korea the day before I left to return to the US.

I have to admit that initially I was not very kind to him on the phone. I just thought that it was another salesman trying to sell me something I really didn't need. When he said, "Don, the last time I saw you and talked to you was in Korea," he had my full attention. I was shocked, jumped up out of my chair and tried my best to remember who he was. It took a while and finally it started to come back to me. He and I had one visit in Korea before I left the next morning to go home.

Paul and his wife, Marilyn, were planning a visit to Grand Junction soon, and we arranged to meet again. The second time we met was a greeting I will never forget! Paul and Marilyn parked on the street in front of our home. Paul walked towards our driveway while Marilyn stood by the car. I walked from our front door to meet Paul on the driveway. Joann stayed at the front door. Paul and I were overcome with emotion at first. It was quite a scene: two men with shared traumatic experiences meeting again after many decades. Paul and I finally broke loose and our wives joined us. We had a nice visit that day that made for a great reunion celebration.

Paul Fulk and me in Colorado. (family photo)

Paul shared his experience of arriving in Korea with the 120th Medical Battalion. His commanding officer greeted him, "You are a CO aren't you?" Paul replied, "Yes, sir." The officer responded, "We got rid of our COs over the past six months, and we do not want any more. Don't unpack your duffel bag, because you will be on the frontlines within three days."

Now as I reflect upon my experience, I believe this officer's attitude accounts for my reassignment from 121 Evac to the frontlines. As a CO, we felt the Army wanted us out of the way. Naturally, Paul dreaded the notion of reporting to the frontline when he recalled the story about an Illinois soldier killed in Korea. Increased ominous thoughts and uncertainties accompanied assignments to the frontlines. As it turned out, Paul never saw that officer again. Rather than a frontline assignment, Paul became an assistant who helped with patients and paperwork at an aid station where he served until he returned home.

Visiting reminded me that being a CO with a frontline assignment seemed like a tremendous trial at the time. Now after much reflection I appreciate the experience. I am glad that I had the opportunity to help a few wounded soldiers get to safety. For me, my frontline experiences continue to provide meaningful satisfaction.

Now the four of us try to attend a church convention together every year. We often talk about Korea, and always talk with the ministers who labor in Korea. Our visits seem as encouraging to us now as the first visit between two young soldiers many years ago.

Chapter 38
Official Korean Recognition

On June 25, 2000, I received the following letter:

Dear Veteran:

On this occasion of the 50th anniversary of the outbreak of the Korean War, I would like to offer you my deepest gratitude for your noble contribution to the effort to safeguard the Republic of Korea and uphold liberal democracy around the world. At the same time, I remember with endless respect and affection those who sacrificed their live for that cause.

We Koreans hold dear in our hearts the conviction, courage and spirit of sacrifice shown to us by such selfless friends as you, who enabled us to remain a free democratic nation.

The ideals of democracy, for which you were willing to sacrifice your all 50 years ago, have become universal values in this new century and millennium.

Half a century after the Korean War, we honor you and reaffirm our friendship, which helped to forge the blood alliance between our two countries. And we resolve once again to work with all friendly nations for the good of humankind and peace in the world.

I thank you once again for your noble sacrifice, and pray for your health and Happiness.

Sincerely yours,

(Signed)

Kim Dae – jung
President of the Republic of Korea

That letter means very much to me!

Chapter 39
Recognition from Grandchildren

My granddaughter, Alexis Den Herder, was asked at school to write an essay about today's patriots. Below is a copy of her paper.

WHO ARE TODAY'S PATRIOTS?

We value our American patriots today because they help establish and protect the freedom of our country. The dictionary defines a patriot as someone who loves his or her country and supports its authority and interests. One close patriot to my life is my grandpa, Don Borgman. He was a soldier and a medic in the American Army serving in Korea from 1951 to 1953 during the Korean War.

My grandpa bravely helped the sick and wounded US troops as a medic. He had many, often frightening, experiences in the American Army. Some experiences were life threatening, many heart rendering, and all were intense and demanding. Going through deep trenches, carrying wounded men, and dodging bombs was really tough. He tells stories about some of the people he helped. Some survived, and some made the ultimate sacrifice by giving their lives for their country. All helped hold the line against tyranny. My grandpa is very interested that countries maintain their freedom.

Many soldiers receive medals for their service. Combat medics are no exception, and my grandpa earned a medal for his courageous combat medic duty. On their discharge papers, the veterans were told their medals would be sent to them later and would arrive after they were discharged. However, because of a government paperwork mix-up, it took over 50 years to receive that medal, and I was with my grandpa when it was presented to him. Retired General Harry Hagaman and Republican Scott McInnis, my Grandpa's local congressman, held a ceremony to honor my grandpa and one other soldier in Grand Junction Colorado, February, 2004. Grandpa appreciated it very much, and he was quoted in the local newspaper saying that he felt honored at the end of the ceremony.

Because my grandfather, Don Borgman, faithfully served the American Army as a medic, he is recognized and valued as an American Patriot. His memories and experiences are both frightening and interesting. At the end of the war, he was awarded a medal for his courage and bravery as a medic. I am proud of my grandpa's service and I am honored to be a patriot's granddaughter. He is proud to be an American, and firmly believes in the causes to protect freedom.

Alexis Den Herder, 2005 (family photo)

Another granddaughter wrote this poem for a school project:

He was on the frontlines
He was a combat medic
He helped injured soldiers
He chose no gun
Others protected him
I will always be proud of him
He is my grandpa

Hannah Den Herder, 2006 (family photo)

Chapter 40
Korean Service Medal

When I received my discharge at Fort Carson on April 5, 1953, I was told that I would receive my Korean Service Medal at a later date. Time went by and I gave it little thought. In 2002 I was asked by a friend, Barbara MacDonald, if I received my Korean Service Medal. I said I had not, and Barbara told of other Korean Veterans, with the help of their local congressmen, who received their medals.

Barbara MacDonald (family photo)

I was encouraged to contact our congressmen and did so immediately. At our appointment, I answered all their questions and went home encouraged that I would finally be given the medal. However, after waiting several months, I did not receive a follow-up response or a medal.

I shared this information with our close friend, Sandy Ragsdale, who sent a letter to Congressman, McInnis. Soon thereafter, I received a call from his office.

Korean Service Medal

Mark Ragsdale, me, Sandy Ragsdale (family photo)

November 11, 2003
Dear Mr. McInnis,

Let me tell you about a man I know. He is probably the most honest, kind, hard working patriotic man I know. Around Veteran's day he comes to stay with my family and me every year to hunt. Maybe it is because it is this particular holiday or maybe because my father had similar experiences but he always ends up reliving his time spent in the service of his country during the Korean War.

Donald Borgman went into the service in 1951 at the age of 18 and trained with the infantry and then as a medic. He remained in the Army until 1953. During that time his records show that he was under enemy fire for 5 months while working on the frontline. He was reported as "Missing In Action" for several months and presumed dead. Many of his experiences were nothing short of heroic and some of his experiences I'm sure we will never know about as they are too painful to speak of aloud.

Despite the hardships he and his family endured, Don always remembers respectfully the honor it was for him to serve his country. To this day he lives near the Walker Field Airport to hear the fighter jets fly in. He says that to him it is the sound of freedom. He has even taken his wife back to Korea to the very battlegrounds he saved lives on.

Only recently a nurse at the Veteran's Hospital asked Don about his Korean Service Medal. He did not receive one and only because of the encouragement from this particular nurse did he go to your office, fill out the paperwork, and wait patiently for the honor he should have received years ago. To date his efforts have been in vain.

On this Veteran's Day I will honor his service to our country and show my appreciation by writing to you about this courageous veteran who deserves the reward of the Korean Service Medal to show his sons, grandsons, and great-grandsons.

Sincerely,

Sandy Ragsdale
Proud American

Soon after Sandy sent this letter to Congressmen McInnis, I was called to answer more questions concerning my medal and my time in the service. Another Korean War veteran and I were awarded our medals 50 years late but I am very happy to have it.

Joann, me, Congressmen McInnis (family photo)

Don and Joann Borgman (family photo)

Acknowledgements

Expressing my thanks for help with this book begins by thanking those who helped me through my experience during the Korean War. Letters from my parents provided tremendous help and encouragement. Letters from our ministers (some of whom I had not previously met) were invaluable. When the letters gave me an address of someone who was finding it difficult to function under war conditions, it gave me a sense of purpose to visit them and try to encourage them.

Writing this book has also truly renewed and amplified my gratitude for the soldiers who helped me. Some supported me during basic and medical training and others helped me with duties in Korea. I am particularly grateful to the soldiers who directly protected me. Many times I was directly exposed to the enemy when I retrieved a wounded soldier. I could hear the mortars leave the barrels of the enemy guns, and my fellow soldiers relentlessly fired their weapons while holding down the enemy. I feel like I owe my survival to these courageous men who took risks on my behalf.

I am very thankful for the support of my family over the years. My gratitude has been felt more keenly as I have worked on this book. I appreciate the interest that has been shown and the help recalling these stories. I would like to express my heartfelt thanks to my son-in-law and daughter, Loren and Sara Den Herder for their willingness to help with this project that is so precious to me. They have provided the good taste and judgment that was needed to turn my memories and experiences into an enjoyable and readable story. This project was of greater magnitude than I had ever imagined it to be in the beginning and without their knowledge, talent, and countless hours of labor, I could never have reached this point. Saying thank you does not begin to scratch the surface of my appreciation for all their help during every phase.

I also want to thank the members of the Women's University Club's creative writing class for their incredibly helpful suggestions. Finally, I sincerely thank the many proofreaders: Ann Borgman, Ben Foster, Diane Simpson, Mary Zosel and Renea Zosel. Their many hours and suggestions have added greatly to the quality of this book.

References

About.Com. (n.d.). *Korean War Pictures.* Retrieved
November 14, 2009 from http://history1900s.
about.com/od/photographs/ig/Korean-War-Pictures
Pictures courtesy of the National Archives and
Records Administration.

Army History. (2002). *Army Military History.* Retrieved
November 14, 2009 from http://www.history
.army.mil/photos/Korea/kor1951/kor1951.htm.
Images are the work of a U.S. Army soldier or
employee, taken or made during the course of the
person's official duties. As a work of the U.S. federal
government, the images are in the public domain.

Army Logistics University. (n.d.). *Artillery Ammunition in the
Korean War.* Retrieved October 3, 2009 from
http://www.almc.army.mil/alog/issues/
SepOct98/MS297.htm

Camp White Military Museum. (n.d.). *A Note About Taps.*
Eagle Point, Oregon. Retrieved September 1, 2008
from <http://www.campwhite.org/cemetery.htm>

CDRS. (n.d.). *Military and Police Salute.* Retrieved November
14, 2009 from http://mycdrs.org/
militarypolicediscounts.aspx

D'Anca, B. and The Baileyville Sesquicentennial Committee.
(2007). *Baileyville, Illinois August 4, 2007
Sesquicentennial.*

Digital History. (2006). *Integrating The Armed Forces.* Retrieved September 26, 2009 from http://www.digitalhistory.uh.edu /historyonline/integrating.cfm

Hickey, M. (1999). *The Korean War.* Woodstock, NY: The Overlook Press, Peter Mayer Publishers, Inc. ISBN 1-58567-035-9. Permissions obtained: From The Korean War copyright © 1999 Michael Hickey. Published in 2000 by The Overlook Press, New York, New York. All rights reserved.

Korean War, The. (1999). United Nations Command Troop Strengths. Retrieved October 3, 2009 from http://www.korean-war.com/unitednations.html

KWVR (Korean War Veteran's Reunion). (March 2006). Mesquite, NV: Transcriptions from the audio recordings and from notes taken during the meetings. http://rkivs.com/kwvr/transcripts.html

Learning Centre, The. (n.d.). *WWI Research Project.* Retrieved November 14, 2009 from http://www.thelearningcentre.org/ww1/ sect3_p1.htm

Macro History. (2001). *Korean War Map.* Retrieved October 3, 2009 from http://www.fsmitha.com /h2/map24ko.html

Office of Insular Affairs. (2004). *Congressional Testimony.* Retrieved October 3, 2009 from http://www. doi.gov/oia/Testimony/72104guam_war_claims.htm

Olive-Drab. (n.d.). *Olive-Drab Military Photos.* Retrieved November 14, 2009 from http://www.Olive-drab.com. These photos are drawn from the immense collections of the U.S. Government in the National Archives, the archives of the military services, and compilations of these photos maintained by universities, libraries and foundations. Such photos are in the public domain and may be used for any lawful purpose.

Paul Noll. (n.d.). *Money from the Korean War.* Retrieved October 3, 2009 from http://www.paulnoll.com /Korea/war-Korea-money-choices.html

PsyWarrior. (2006). *Communist North Korea War Leaflets.* Retrieved November 14, 2009 from http://www.psywarrior.com/NKoreaH.html

PJ Lighthouse. (n.d.). *Courage is not the absence of fear.* Retrieved October 3, 2009 from http://www.pjlighthouse.com/category/quotes/

Song, J. H. (1952). *Glimpses of Korea.* Korea: International Publicity League of Korea.

Terrell, H. (2004). *Heroes Among Us.* Victoria, BC, Canada: Trafford Publishing. ISBN 1-4120-1108-6.

The New Medic. (1951). *Medical Replacement Training Center Yearbook.* Fort George G. Meade, Maryland. N.Y.C. Yearbook Publishing Co., Inc.

Vigilant Hunter Brigade. (n.d.). *A Brief History of Military Medics.* Retrieved October 3, 2009 from http://www.vhbusa.com/medicteam.html

4415132

Made in the USA
Lexington, KY
23 January 2010